THE UNITED STATES
AND THE
GLOBAL ECONOMY

THE UNITED STATES AND THE GLOBAL ECONOMY

From Bretton Woods to the Current Crisis

Frederick S. Weaver

ROWMAN & LITTLEFIELD PUBLISHERS, INC.
Lanham • Boulder • New York • Toronto • Plymouth, UK

Published by Rowman & Littlefield Publishers, Inc.
A wholly owned subsidiary of The Rowman & Littlefield Publishing Group, Inc.
4501 Forbes Boulevard, Suite 200, Lanham, Maryland 20706
http://www.rowmanlittlefield.com

Estover Road, Plymouth PL6 7PY, United Kingdom

British Library Cataloguing in Publication Information Available

Library of Congress Cataloging-in-Publication Data

Weaver, Frederick Stirton, 1939–
  The United States and the global economy : from Bretton Woods to the
current crisis / Frederick S. Weaver.
      p. cm.
  Includes bibliographical references and index.
  ISBN 978-1-4422-0889-6 (cloth : alk. paper) — ISBN 978-1-4422-0890-2
(electronic)
  1. United States—Foreign economic relations. 2. United States—Commerce.
3. United States—Economic conditions—1945– 4. United States—Economic
policy. I. Title.
  HF1455.W3174 2011
  337.73—dc23
                                                                2011027704

∞™ The paper used in this publication meets the minimum requirements of
American National Standard for Information Sciences—Permanence of Paper
for Printed Library Materials, ANSI/NISO Z39.48-1992.

Printed in the United States of America

For
Sharon Hartman Strom

Contents

Acknowledgments

I have been privileged to be a Reader at the Huntington Library in Pasadena, California, for two periods during the writing of this book. The Huntington gave me a place to work, world-class resources, and a set of outstanding and congenial colleagues in an extraordinarily beautiful setting. The Huntington has to be one of the most delightful places to work (and wander) in the world. Within the Huntington, I am especially grateful to the staff of the Readers Services Department for their helpfulness, courtesy, and humor. The welcoming of the residential community at Monte Vista Grove Homes and the assistance of Nancy Lain and Ed Cortez have helped make my stays in Pasadena both pleasant and productive. I am also grateful to my Rowman & Littlefield editors, Niels Aaboe, Carrie Broadwell-Tkach, Sarah David, and Jehanne Schweitzer, for their encouragement and support.

My greatest debt, however, is to my wife, Sharon Hartman Strom. She contributed mightily to this book with suggestions about substance and presentation and with good judgment and humor and wonderful companionship at a time when she had her own projects in the works.

Thank you all.

Introduction

This book introduces readers to the patterns of change in the international economy since World War II. These patterns, I argue, have profound implications within nations for shifts in political power, income distribution, workers' rights, and social and welfare policies. The organization of the book is generally chronological, but the reader will find that the chronology becomes rather elastic at times in order to complete an argument or to tie up a loose end. The international economy is constantly changing and developing, and this approach is appropriate for deepening our understanding of recent global economic turmoil.

The speed of such changes can be dizzying. For example, the international economic crisis beginning in 2008 was itself a game changer for domestic politics and international relations. While people were trying to dig themselves out from the morass of the Great Recession, political upheavals in North Africa and the Middle East occurred in early 2011, along with an earthquake and tsunami in Japan that caused a potential nuclear catastrophe. These are momentous events that will continue to affect the international economy in myriad ways, but since these events occurred as I was finishing this book and continued to unfold as I did finish it, they can appear in my narrative only as bare sketches, but, I hope, evocative ones.

1

The ways in which international events, issues, and relationships reflected and shaped changes in the U.S. economy is my central theme. This attention to the United States is not simple jingoism; over the last sixty years, the United States has been the dominant player in the world economy, and although its dominance is not as complete as it once was, the U.S. government's actions and economic processes still have definite effects on global economic affairs, for better and for worse. There have been a number of international developments that have affected the U.S. role in the international economy and that are important in their own right: the emergence of the European Union, policies of the Organization of Petroleum Exporting Countries, the collapse of the Soviet Union, the rise of China as an export superpower, and economic successes in South Korea, India, Brazil, and Southeast Asia. Each of these has to be considered carefully.

A second goal of this book is to provide the reader with the vocabulary of key elements of international economic analysis and their interactions, with the hope of making international economic affairs more accessible. It is difficult to understand news accounts of international economic happenings without grasping the differences between balances of trade and balances of payments, foreign direct investment and foreign portfolio investment, or the meaning of most-favored-nation agreements.

The chapters' emphases go back and forth between the international economy and the U.S. economy to illustrate their interactions. After a brief look at U.S. involvement in the international economy before World War II, chapter 1 describes the Bretton Woods conference of 1944, the dollar exchange standard, and the three international institutions created to monitor and guide the new international structure. Although not a direct result of the Bretton Woods agreement, the European Economic Community, established in 1957, was the fourth major economic institution created in the two decades after World War II.

Chapter 2 focuses on features of the U.S. economy that came together in the 1950s and 1960s with implications for the nation and the world. The new type of transnational corporation was a product of that new configuration, changing patterns of international trade and politics throughout the Cold War world by drawing many less-industrialized countries into the international economy in new ways.

Chapter 3 records the success of the dollar exchange standard in expanding international trade and investment, and how the ensuing prosperity facilitated new shifts in U.S. politics. The very success of the Bretton Woods system caused its own destruction by undermining the strength of the U.S. dollar in the face of an increasingly competitive international economy. When the U.S. government unilaterally abrogated the Bretton Woods agreement in 1971, the consequent devaluation of the dollar triggered the quadrupling of petroleum prices and, in turn, the 1980s international debt crises in less-developed countries.

Chapter 4 returns to the U.S. economy, emphasizing the ways in which increased price competition from foreign firms disrupted relations among U.S. firms and between employers and workers, and impeded the further development of social policies. The new competitive patterns also recast the international economy. After describing the dynamics of the new free-market global capitalism, I discuss the ways in which the changed patterns created new transnational corporate behavior and a surge of deregulation initiatives.

Chapter 5 continues the fourth chapter's line of reasoning by exploring the manner in which free-market global capitalism affected the traditional relationship between inflation and unemployment, the balance-of-trade conundrum, the efficacy of domestic fiscal and monetary stabilization policies, and the distribution of income. The chapter next poses the question of whether trading blocs such as the European Union, the North American Free Trade Area, and Mercosur promote or retard the development of free-trade global capitalism, and it concludes with the emergence of new trading partners, with particular attention to China, India, and Brazil.

Chapter 6 addresses the stability of free-trade global capitalism. It begins with an analysis of the role of speculative capital, flowing throughout the world in the pursuit of short-term gains, and the ways in which it destabilized currencies and financial systems in Europe, Mexico, and East and Southeast Asia. The second section of the chapter examines the financial collapse of 2008 and 2009 in the United States, which revealed profound weaknesses in other parts of the global economy. The chapter ends with a somber view of the steps being taken and not being taken to put national economies on a sound path of economic growth with a more generous sharing of material benefits.

I have addressed some of these international economic issues in previous publications, most notably the last chapter of my *Economic Literacy: Basic Economics with an Attitude* (Rowman & Littlefield, 2011). In this book, I have expanded, clarified, and reframed my previous writings in ways that I believe are accessible, provocative, and interesting. But of course I would think so.

1

The Twentieth-Century Quest for a Stable International Economy

By the end of the nineteenth century, Native Americans who had survived the European invasions, disease, and rough treatment had been forced onto reservations. The Chinese Exclusion Act of 1888 prohibited most immigration from China. Many African Americans were living under Jim Crow laws, enforced by terror and lynching, that severely limited their mobility and opportunities. The rights of Mexican Americans, many of whom were descended from families who had been in California, Arizona, New Mexico, and Texas for generations, were severely circumscribed. Even Irish, Italian, and Central and Eastern European immigrants—whites, no less—were treated with scorn.

These parochial and intolerant sensibilities were not unique to the United States, but they do not suggest a people eager to engage the world with all of its multiplicity. Nevertheless, if the British and French, with their fiercely held convictions of racial and cultural superiority, could rule empires on which the sun never set, there also were possibilities for the chauvinistic United States. But the U.S. engagement with the world was not a smoothly increasing flow of connections; it went forward in fits and starts and, with a couple of exceptions, began seriously only after World War II.

Setting the Stage: The United States and the International Economy before 1944

The nineteenth-century United States simply did not need much from the rest of the world. By the middle of the century, the Louisiana Purchase (1803), the acquisition of Texas (1845), and the Mexican War (1846–1848) had made the United States into a continent-wide free-trade zone with a rapidly growing population, rich soils, and abundant forests and mineral deposits. As a result, the United States had only slight dependence on exports for markets and imports for essential products.

Agricultural exports made up about 20 percent of U.S. agricultural output, led by wheat, cotton, and meat—that last with improved refrigeration in the last quarter of the century. But total exports (and imports) represented only around 6 percent of U.S. gross national product through the nineteenth century, while European nations exported 20 to 30 percent of their total production.[1]

The major news about U.S. exports and imports was the significant change in their composition in the late nineteenth and early twentieth centuries, reflecting the prodigious expansion and maturation of the U.S. industrial sector. Table 1.1 records

Table 1.1. The Changing Composition of Nineteenth-Century U.S. Exports and Imports

A. Type of Exports as a Proportion of Total Exports			
	Raw Materials and Unprocessed Food	Manufactured Goods and Processed Food	Total
1850–1858	67.3	32.8	100.0
1904–1913	40.0	59.9	100.0
B. Type of Imports as a Proportion of Total Imports			
	Raw Materials and Unprocessed Food	Manufactured Goods and Processed Food	Total
1850–1858	19.9	80.1	100.0
1904–1913	46.5	53.6	100.0

Source: Robert E. Lipsey, "U.S. Foreign Trade and the Balance of Payments, 1800–1913," in The Cambridge Economic History of the United States, vol. 2, The Long Nineteenth Century, ed. Stanley L. Engerman and Robert E. Gallman (New York: Cambridge University Press, 2000), 702.

that by the early twentieth century, the U.S. role in world trade had largely shifted away from being an exporter of resource-based ("primary") products and importer of manufactured ("secondary") products. The export and import of services ("tertiary products") such as tourism, insurance, and other financial products would become more significant during the second half of the twentieth century.

In contrast to trade—imports and exports—European (mostly British) investments into the United States were large and crucial, especially for canal and railroad construction and for urban infrastructure such as water and sewer systems. By the beginning of the twentieth century, U.S. investors had begun to invest more abroad than foreigners invested in the United States. Despite this change, the net balance of accumulated foreign investments—the total value of foreign investments in the United States minus the total value of U.S. investments abroad—was still $2.6 billion in 1914. But U.S. involvement in the broader world of the nineteenth century went beyond trade and investment.

The Era of Heroic Adventures

In the second half of the nineteenth century, the United States aggressively fashioned new commercial opportunities and acquired new territories outside North America. But the U.S. drive for new colonies did not come close to that of the Europeans, who had colonized virtually all of Africa, South Asia, and Southeast Asia by World War I.

From the seventeenth century, the Chinese, Japanese, and Korean governments discouraged most contacts with Western governments and merchants. In the 1850s, Great Britain allied with France, the United States, and Russia and forced the weak Chinese government to open trade with the four nations' merchants. And in the 1850s, a U.S. naval squadron commanded by Commodore Matthew C. Perry sailed into the harbor of Edo (Tokyo), demanded trading rights, and shelled a portion of the city. The bullying worked, and Perry eventually obtained a trade treaty with the Japanese government.

But there was a backlash within Japan. The Japanese military and some merchants and landed aristocrats were enraged at the unequal terms of the trade agreement, and in 1868 they overthrew the Japanese government in what is known as the Meiji Restoration. The new leaders resolved to learn from the West in order to defend themselves against westerners. Japan's defeat of Russia in the Russo-Japanese War (1904–1905) dramatically heralded Japan's success in establishing a modern industrial sector and military powerhouse that was to become a formidable imperialist competitor of the Western powers in East Asia.

In contrast, the United States Navy tried to "open" Korea in 1871 in a manner similar to that of Japan, but it was notoriously unsuccessful. Korea remained secluded until taken over by Japan in 1905 and made into a Japanese colony in 1910.

The U.S. government annexed the Hawaiian Islands as a U.S. territory in 1898, finally acceding to the continuing entreaties of Hawaii's white minority. The whites had taken over the Hawaiian government in an 1863 coup supported by U.S. sailors and marines, but they were fearful of the nonwhite Hawaiian majority as well as Japan's interest in the islands. Annexation by the United States would solve both these problems as well as ensure that Hawaii never could be closed out of the U.S. sugar market. Although Hawaii had a white government deliberately modeled on the U.S. South that effectively disenfranchised the nonwhite majority—mostly native Hawaiians, Japanese, and Chinese—there was considerable resistance in the U.S. Congress to annexing nonwhite populations. The supporters of annexation in the U.S. Senate were not sure that they had the votes, so they used a possibly illegal legislative maneuver to circumvent the usual two-thirds vote in the Senate needed to ratify such a treaty.

In the Caribbean, a third Cuban War of Independence against Spanish colonial control began in 1895. A mixed bag of real brutalities wildly exaggerated by U.S. press reports generated sympathy for the Cuban independence effort in the United States. In one of the triggers to U.S. involvement, the U.S. cruiser *Maine* mysteriously exploded in Havana harbor in February 1898, and the tragedy was widely but erroneously blamed on the Spaniards. Economic motivations (sugar) and strategic agendas (a naval coaling station) also played a role, and the United States entered the war in April 1898. The war ended ten weeks later.

The Treaty of Paris, signed at the end of the same year, awarded the United States the former Spanish colonies of Puerto Rico, Guam, and the Philippine Islands, designating Cuba as a U.S. protectorate. The Treaty of Paris was highly unpopular with broad sectors of the U.S. electorate; the population of the Philippines—seven million Filipinos of Negrito, Malay, Indonesian, and European descent—was a major stumbling block. The treaty was ratified by the U.S. Senate on February 6, 1899, by a margin of one ballot even though the vote had been preceded by exceptionally large flows of legal tender, federal judgeships, and other favors directed at senators and their families.

In Cuba, the United States successfully demobilized the Cuban liberation army, but it was another matter in the Philippines. The Filipino liberation army regarded the U.S. military as allies in their war of independence against Spain, and the liberation army cleared most of the islands of what had always been a slight Spanish presence outside Manila. It was a shock when the Treaty of Paris declared the Philippines a colony of the United States, and the liberation army fought back.

It took seventy thousand U.S. troops until 1903 to conquer the Philippines in a nasty guerrilla war complete with burning villages, looting, and general butchery by both sides. The final death tolls were around 4,200 U.S. soldiers, 20,000 Filipino soldiers, and 200,000 Filipino civilians.

In the early twentieth century, the United States continued to demonstrate interest in affairs beyond its borders. It gained sovereignty over a ten-mile strip across Panama's isthmus for a canal in 1903, invaded Haiti and the Dominican Republic to limit European bondholders' influence, and entered World War I in 1917, almost two and a half years after it began.

On the home front, the first two decades of the century also saw a revival of the Progressive Era's reform agenda, and constitutional amendments allowed an income tax, prohibited the production and sale of alcoholic beverages, and enfranchised women. Separate legislation strengthened financial regulation and consumer protections and prohibited child labor and monopolies exercising their power by raising prices.

Retreat from the International Economy—Fascist Europe and Soviet Russia

In order to finance World War I, Great Britain and France borrowed heavily from U.S. public and private lenders and also drew down their investments in the United States. Between 1914 and 1919, U.S. investment abroad rose by more than two and a half times and foreign investment in the United States declined almost 25 percent, giving the United States a net international credit balance of $8.5 billion. The United States had gone from the world's largest international net debtor to the largest international net creditor in five years.

The Treaty of Versailles at the end of World War I redrew the map of Europe by dissolving the empires of the losing Central Powers—the German Empire, the Austro-Hungarian Empire, and the Ottoman Empire— establishing new nations, granting German colonies to the French and British, and distributing sizable pieces of the former empires and Bulgaria to neighboring nations. Table 1.2 lists the major changes in borders and nations.

In the negotiations around the Versailles Treaty, France, Belgium, and other allies, under pressure to repay their $10 billion wartime debt to public and private U.S. creditors, led a successful effort to impose draconian war reparations on the Germans of £6.6 billion as well as on other Central Power belligerents. These payments caused hyperinflation in Germany and throughout Central and Eastern Europe and severe deterioration of already weakened economies.

These economic stresses added to general instability, complete with regionwide insurrectionary and interethnic turmoil, exacerbated by the Great Depression after 1930. The consequence was a fertile field for the growth of fascism, and by 1939 every nation in Southern, Central, and Eastern Europe,

Table 1.2. Changing National Landscapes after World War I

Central Powers	After World War I
German Empire	Important pieces of the empire granted to Poland and France; small pieces to Denmark, Belgium, and Czechoslovakia; colonies to the United Kingdom, France, and the United States (a few small Pacific islands).
Austro-Hungarian Empire	Broken into the nations of Austria, Hungary, Czechoslovakia, and Yugoslavia; important parts of the old empire granted to Poland, Italy, and Romania.
Ottoman Empire	Limited to Turkey (Anatolia, Istanbul, and a small piece on the European side of the Bosporus). France received control of Syria, Lebanon, and Jordan; the United Kingdom received control of Palestine; decades of turmoil in the Arabian Peninsula finally yield Saudi Arabia, Yeman, Oman, and some small emirates.
Bulgaria	No major changes.
Allied Powers	
Russian Empire (Soviet Union)	Finland, Lithuania, Latvia, Estonia, Armenia, Georgia, and Azerbaijan established as independent from Russia, but within two decades all but Finland become part of the Soviet Union.

with the exception of Czechoslovakia, followed the lead of Italy and established strongly nationalist right-wing authoritarian governments that were fascist, protofascist, or semifascist. They brutally smashed labor movements and any hint of socialism or communism. The 1933 election of Adolf Hitler graphically illustrated the desperation of the era.

These nationalist governments pursued an economic policy of autarky—self-sufficiency. They went off the gold standard, repudiated foreign debt and reparation payments, and centralized and militarized political power, often at the expense of the large industrialists and landowners who initially supported them. Japan underwent a similar process when the Japanese military, allied with important big-business interests, destroyed the last vestiges of political moderation in the 1930s.

The 1917 communist revolution in Russia led to Soviet policies similar to fascist strategies in that they aspired to autarky, and in the early years of the revolution, Vladimir Lenin's New Economic Policy combined private and government ownership. This nuanced approach ended with Lenin's 1924 death, the ascendance of Joseph Stalin, and the First Five-Year Plan (1928–1933) that inaugurated almost complete state control and central planning in the economy.

The principal goal of the Five-Year Plans was the creation of a modern industrial sector that could supply the materiel to defend the Soviet Union against an expected invasion by the capitalist nations. After all, around 120,000 troops from Japan, Greece, France, Great Britain, and the United States, along with thousands from other anti-Soviet governments, had invaded Russia in the early 1920s in an unsuccessful attempt to destroy the Bolshevik state.

Collectivization of agriculture was an integral part of the drive to industrialization. The effort began in the 1920s, and by 1935 more than 90 percent of cultivated land was in collective farms. Four to ten million people died in the process and associated shortages and diseases, and tens of thousands were imprisoned or deported to Siberia. The ostensible purpose of collectivization was to modernize Russian agriculture through mechanization, and while that goal was not very successful, two other less-publicized goals were. Collectivization crushed rural and peasant resistance to the Soviet regime, and it enabled the Soviets to construct a centrally controlled mechanism to squeeze produce and potential factory workers out of agriculture to support the industrialization drive.

The Soviet industrial sector grew rapidly in a decade, paid for by agricultural workers and consumers in general. The industrialization was of heavy industry, and between 1928 and 1938, steel production increased four times and truck and tractor production rose by one hundred times. On the other hand, such consumer products as clothing barely kept up with population growth, although standards of living did rise somewhat in urban areas. And this industrial development occurred during the Great Depression, in which the capitalist world continued to be mired.

Retreat from the International Economy—
Semi-industrialized Nations

Those nations that were principally exporters of primary products but had become partially industrialized with substantial urban populations constituted another type of autarkic response. Unlike Central American nations that were small and rural and simply contracted during the Depression, the larger and more advanced national economies of Latin America, Turkey, Egypt, Thailand, and even British India could not shrink without radical social and political transformations. The local business class of producers and retailers, the urban working class, and a nascent middle class of public and private white-collar employees were not likely to slink quietly away into subsistence agriculture. A sudden and severe decline of these urban groups' standards of living would have torn apart the more complex nations.

These national governments did not deliberately retreat from international markets. The collapse of primary commodity markets in the 1930s was so devastating that international markets simply were no longer available, and governments had little choice but to go off the gold standard, renege on foreign loans, and turn inward to protect their urban economies and maintain the political support of urban constituencies, especially the urban working classes that would not suffer high rates of unemployment without public protests and violent resistance. The very conditions that made this policy shift to inward development imperative also made it feasible; the political position of traditional elites, based on their control of traditional exports, was so badly eroded from the loss of foreign markets that their domestic political influence was severely weakened.

The result was that these nations instituted a defensive set of emergency economic policies subsequently known as "import-substituting industrialization." The term is descriptive: substituting local industrial production for goods that formerly had been imported. This was the path that the United States and Germany chose in their nineteenth-century industrialization behind high tariff walls. The semi-industrialized countries, with their governments facing the possibility of major urban unemployment and insurrection, used tariffs but also a range of other mechanisms to manage their relationships with the international economy. Two such measures were the use of physical quotas on imports and currency controls, which are government monopolies on foreign currency holdings with the aim of allocating foreign currency only to the buying of imports deemed to be of the highest priority. In addition, governments of these nations often took over or at least carefully regulated activities considered crucial to the domestic economy. These included utilities, railroads, steel production, petroleum refining, and often entire financial sectors. The loss of revenue from export taxes pushed these governments into fiscal deficits, which supported domestic demand to the point that several of them were experiencing inflation while the leading industrial nations were struggling with deflation.

Retreat from International Involvement—
Industrialized Democracies

In the United States of the 1920s, there was a sharp division, even contradiction, between the outsized U.S. participation in international trade and finance and a political reaction in the United States against participation in international affairs outside the Americas. This isolationism was clear when the U.S. Congress refused to join President Woodrow Wilson's vision of a League of Nations. Subsequent Republican-dominated Congresses and the administrations of Presidents Warren Harding, Calvin Coolidge, and Herbert Hoover, appalled by continuing and potentially violent quarrels among European nations, raised tariffs in 1920, 1921, and 1930, placed more restrictions on immigration, prohibited official U.S. participation in international conferences, and stepped away from the potential risks, obligations, and rewards of the U.S. dollar becoming the key international currency.

The isolationism of the 1920s complemented a reversed course in domestic politics. The common portrayal of the 1920s as the "Roaring Twenties"—a carefree time of jazz, flappers,

Prohibition-era speakeasies, fast cars, and gangsters—masks the political and economic difficulties of the decade. Passage of the Nineteenth Amendment enfranchising women in 1920 was not the harbinger of new reforms but the last major reform for a decade. The Red Scare and anti-Bolshevik domestic crackdowns were reactions to the Russian Revolution and enabled the U.S. government to use the Espionage and Sedition Acts passed during the patriotic fervor of World War I to deport immigrants active in the U.S. labor movement, crush the wave of postwar strikes, and deter political dissidence in general.

Post–World War I attempts by Western Europe and the United States to bring back the international gold standard were not successful, and the Great Depression of the 1930s wiped away attempts to restore international commerce and investment on a pre–World War I footing. In the 1930s, international commerce declined around half due to reduced demand and to national governments' use of tariffs, quotas, exchange controls, and competitive devaluations to stimulate their domestic economies at the expense of trading partners.

The U.S. and Western European governments adhered to the conventional thinking that governments should balance their budgets to create a stable monetary environment and little else in the way of macroeconomic policy. By relying on market mechanisms, the standard analysis went, the Depression would eventually drive wages and prices down to the point that employers would resume hiring and consumers would once again purchase goods and services. One problem was that the deflation was uneven. Between 1929 and 1934, agricultural prices in the United States declined over 50 percent from already depressed post–World War I prices, while prices of manufactured goods, which operated in less competitive markets, declined less than 20 percent. A second problem was that producers would not resume hiring until there was adequate demand for their products, and consumers would not resume buying consumer goods and services unless they had adequate income from employment and production. The chicken-and-egg aspect of this has had recurring historical consequences.

When it became clear in the first three or four years of the Depression that the traditional prescription was not working, the United States and Western Europe, as opposed to the rest of Europe, moved toward social democracy by actively incorporating labor movements into politics and creating social insurance, relief programs, pensions, and other supports for their hard-pressed citizens. World War II brought the United States and Western Europe out of the Depression, and the exigencies of prosecuting the war led to direct government controls over domestic and international commerce.

World War II destroyed large portions of manufacturing capacity and transportation infrastructure in all the major industrialized nations except the United States, which expanded its manufacturing capabilities under tight federal wartime controls and regulations. In 1939 the U.S. economy had been about one-half the size of the combined economies of Europe, Japan, and the Soviet Union. Ten years later, it was larger than those combined economies. The resulting economic and military strength of the United States enabled the U.S. government to assert a new determination to shape international affairs in the post–World War II world.

The Bretton Woods Conference: A Framework for the International Economy

As World War II began, the Allies started to think about an international financial framework robust enough to support a vigorous postwar expansion of international trade and investment. When an Allied victory became imminent, U.S. Treasury Department officials convened a 1944 international conference in Bretton Woods, New Hampshire, with representatives of forty-three Allied nations, one neutral—Argentina—and a handful from European colonies in Africa, South Asia, and Southeast Asia. U.S. Treasury officials and a British representative, John Maynard Keynes, were the principal architects of the new international framework, which was approved by the conference.

Except for the Soviet representatives, who attended Bretton Woods but decided not to join the new pact, there were some general areas of agreement among the principal representatives. One was that international trade and investment were mutually beneficial for all participants. The specific case for international trade is called the theory of comparative advantage (or comparative costs), and David Ricardo presented a precise formulation in his *Principles of Political Economy and Taxation* (1817). Ricardo's theorizing had a very practical application; the theory of comparative advantage was one of the major arguments in British manufacturers' successful effort to abolish British tariffs on imported grain (the "Corn Laws") in 1846. The basics of the modern theory of comparative advantage have not changed much since Ricardo's time.

Units of Analysis and Free Trade

As most introductory economics textbooks will assure you, the argument for the benefits of international specialization and trade among nations is parallel to the argument that specialization among individuals within a nation leads to mutually beneficial exchange. It is true that the theory of comparative advantage does treat nations as indivisible units, comparable to a (nonschizophrenic) individual. But the reality is that nations are not harmonious collections of individuals; they are filled with groups with often conflicting and contradictory interests. This means that a nation does not benefit or lose through international commerce but rather that some groups in the nation benefit at the expense of others. To deny that complexity is to risk conclusions that serve some groups and disadvantage other groups. It may indeed be possible for winners to gain enough to compensate losers and still be ahead, but how likely would political mechanisms be able to achieve such compensation? Arithmetic models based on relative prices and national units are not adequate for an honest analysis of the benefits from international trade and who receives those benefits.

A second area of commonality was that political and economic elites of the leading capitalist nations had experienced a general loss of confidence in the ability of unregulated markets to generate stability and prosperity. This signaled a new willingness to rely on discretionary policies by public authorities. The New Deal and World War II controls demonstrated that active government policies of regulation and demand management could stabilize capitalist economies and that such interventions were necessary for the health of the capitalist system.

Skepticism about the efficacy of unregulated markets included doubting the usefulness of the gold standard and fluctuating exchange rates, free-market adjustment mechanisms to rectify imbalances in a nation's exports and imports—the balance of trade. The gold standard and fluctuating exchange rates occupy opposite ends of an array of possible adjustment mechanisms.

The Gold Standard

The gold standard was the adjustment mechanism that more or less prevailed during most of the nineteenth century and into the early decades of the twentieth. The rules of the gold standard required that gold be the ultimate medium of international exchange and that a nation's money supply be directly linked to the volume of gold, and occasionally silver, that it possessed. Therefore, a nation that imported more goods and services than it exported experienced net outflows of gold that contracted the domestic money supply and reduced the price level of the deficit nation. The resulting deflation made the nation's exports more competitive in international markets because their prices, in both domestic and foreign currencies, had declined, and the deflation made imports less competitive in local markets, because domestic goods' prices had declined while the prices of imports had not.

This double whammy—increasing exports and decreasing imports—thus eased the import-export imbalance. The mirror image was that a nation that exported more than it imported received net inflows of gold that expanded its domestic money supply, and the consequent inflation made imports less expensive in its domestic market and its exports more expensive in foreign markets. Both of these effects moved the surplus nation's exports and imports closer to a balance. The gold standard adjustment mechanism that brought exports and imports into some rough equivalence worked through changes in the price levels of both deficit and surplus nations without any change in exchange rates (the prices of one currency in terms of other currencies, but see the sidebar).

Exchange Rates and Standards of Living

Although exchange rates are indeed the prices at which currencies are converted into others, it is very tricky to use them to compare income figures. That is, if we know the per capita income of Mexico for 2010 (in pesos) and we know the per capita income in the United States for 2010 (in dollars), current exchange rates are not a reliable way to convert them into a common currency in order to compare them. Exchange rates are determined primarily by the markets of international transactions and do not necessarily reflect the actual prices of goods and services produced and consumed locally. Think about how tenuous the relationship is between the exchange rate for the Saudi Arabian currency (the riyal) and the prices of the goods and services most important to most Saudi citizens. There is a school of thought in economics that argues that in the long run exchange rates do tend toward a level that expresses relative costs of living in different nations (the purchasing power parity doctrine), but it is not clear how helpful it is even if true. The World Bank creates separate indices for converting and comparing national income figures.

The actual operation of the gold standard was uncertain, but even when it did work with textbook tidiness, neither inflation nor deflation makes a government popular with citizens. Moreover, governments did not like to abdicate the determination of their domestic money supplies and domestic credit availability to the vicissitudes of international trade and investment or to the serendipity of major gold strikes (causing worldwide inflation) and shortages (exerting deflationary drags).

Flexible Exchange Rates

The principal theoretical alternative to the gold standard is a very different, even polar method of adjustment. A flexible exchange rate system operates through the international demand for and supply of national currencies that have no direct connections with gold. In international currency markets, the supply of the currency of a nation that was importing more than it was exporting would exceed the demand for it, causing that currency's price in respect to other currencies to be driven down by market forces. This devaluation would reduce the price of the deficit nation's exports in foreign markets, encouraging more exports, and raise the price of imports in domestic markets, discouraging imports.

Both these processes would propel the nation closer to balance. The equal and opposite would happen for nations that exported more than they imported. The scarcity of those surplus nations' currencies in international markets would cause a rise (appreciation, or revaluation) of its exchange rate, which in turn would raise the price of its exports in foreign markets, discouraging exports, and reduce the price of imports in domestic markets, encouraging imports.

So like the gold standard, the flexible exchange rate adjustment mechanism worked symmetrically on both deficit and surplus nations, but unlike the gold standard, it relied on changes in exchange rates rather than in national price levels.

The Dollar Exchange Standard

The experiences of the 1920s and 1930s demonstrated the futility of exhuming the nineteenth-century gold standard, and in any case, the successive deflations and inflations by which the gold standard maintained some sort of equivalence between exports and imports among trading nations had become riskier. The 1930s demonstrated that in advanced industrial nations, deflation was not just a neutral, uniform reduction in price levels; even when it occurred, the market power of large manufacturing corporations created a downward stickiness of manufactured product prices that led to contractions of output, a rise in unemployment, and the creation of political difficulties. Inflation also had inconvenient economic and political costs. On the other hand, flexible exchange rate systems sounded too much like the competitive devaluations and exchange rate volatility that had contributed to international economic instability during the 1930s.

Under the Bretton Woods system, also known as the dollar exchange standard, the U.S. dollar became the new key currency—essentially an international legal tender—to which all other currencies would be pegged and defended by their governments. For foreign central banks, dollars were convertible to gold at thirty-five dollars an ounce, and a nation's money supply was independent of its holdings of gold.

The new framework essentially substituted the United States and the U.S. dollar for the role that Great Britain and the British pound performed in the nineteenth century, but the principal Bretton Woods innovations were to break the link between gold and the volume of national money and to create two new international financial institutions: the International Monetary Fund (IMF) and the International Bank for Reconstruction and Development (subsequently known as the World Bank). These two new institutions were charged with monitoring and stabilizing the international trade and payments system.

Anxieties about a potential loss of national sovereignty, especially by the U.S. government, vetoed formation of the International Trade Organization, which Bretton Woods had established to reduce trade barriers. In place of the International Trade Organization, the signatory nations in 1947 created the General Agreement on Tariffs and Trade (GATT), which served as a venue for negotiating reductions of barriers to the international trade of nonagricultural goods.

In the next chapter, I will describe the GATT's mechanisms and effects, and here I will focus on the three other new international institutions designed to work with the reorganized international economy: the IMF, the World Bank, and the European Economic Community, all of which strongly influenced the shape and development of the world economy.

The International Monetary Fund and the World Bank

The responsibility of both the IMF and the World Bank was to work with nations experiencing deficits in their international accounts. Although the functions of the IMF and the World Bank overlapped in the 1980s and 1990s, there was initially a discernible division of labor between them. The IMF's primary responsibility was to deal with imbalances considered to be of a short-term, cyclical nature. It did this by allowing a deficit nation to withdraw in hard currency (for example, U.S. dollars) the equivalent of its IMF "quota" (a country's assessment paid into the IMF, almost a deposit). And a nation could borrow beyond its quota in order to defend its exchange rate and weather a payments deficit without taking actions considered inimical to the international economic structure. Borrowing beyond one's quota, however, often required the borrowing government to agree to certain conditions—the IMF's "conditionality."

Similar to the medicine of the gold standard, the IMF's standard prescriptions to reduce a balance-of-trade deficit have consistently been deflationary domestic policies. The specific target has been reductions in government expenditures, usually such as social services and subsidized food and urban transportation. The IMF saw these reductions as the most effective means to reduce domestic incomes, wages, and inflation in deficit nations. This in turn was thought to lower the offending nations' domestic demand for imports and the prices of their exports, making them more competitive in international markets. In addition, the IMF strongly pressured nations to abolish government regulations such as workers' protections and controls over domestic and international merchandise and financial transactions, including international investment, seen by the IMF as impeding the operation of efficient markets.

Now it is time for a couple of formal definitions. As already mentioned, the balance of trade is the balance between exports and imports of goods and services. It is the principal component of the Current Account, which also contains unilateral transfers (for example, U.S. government grants to foreign militaries and private U.S. residents' remittances to folks in the old country) as well as repatriated earnings from foreign investment (profits from foreign-owned enterprises operating in the United States sent out of the country and profits from U.S.-owned foreign enterprises brought into the country).

The Current Account is in turn a major component of the balance of payments, which is the most comprehensive measure of international transactions. The Capital Account is the second major component, and it records the financial transactions involved in foreign investment. Foreign investment can take myriad forms. When foreigners purchase financial assets such as bank deposits, bonds, derivatives, options, and minor holdings of foreign corporations' stock, it is called foreign portfolio investment. On the other hand, when foreigners purchase "real" assets, such as a cement plant, an auto repair shop, or some farmland in another country, it is called foreign direct investment, which is more often the source of disagreements with foreign governments and firms than foreign portfolio investment that does not control productive resources.

Despite this simplified description of the balance-of-trade adjustment mechanism, it is imperative to recognize that the demand for a nation's currency is not exclusively for buying that nation's exports; it also can be used to invest in that country. IMF prescriptions tend to aim narrowly at imports and exports (the balance of trade) and ignore international flows of investment, which could offset whatever positive changes might occur in the balance of trade. Forcing a deficit nation into a recession discourages new international investment, and abolishing restrictions on capital movements, one of the IMF's frequent recommendations, enables foreigners to divest funds and local residents to engage in capital flight—sending liquid assets abroad to avoid local recessions and risks. These actions pull funds out of the weak economy and push the capital account into deficit. The effects of deflation and deregulation could exacerbate balance-of-payments deficits even if the balance of trade turned positive.

The World Bank, in contrast to the IMF, made long-term loans to countries where chronic balance-of-payments deficits were seen to be due to the very structure of the deficit nation's economy. The purpose of these loans was not to tide the nation over a temporary shortfall of international receipts. The World Bank was to help nations change the domestic composition of their production, create new patterns of comparative advantage, become more competitive internationally, and thus bring their international payments into balance.

The United Nations, also founded in 1944, was another important postwar international organization, but its influence on the world economy has always been less than that of the IMF and the World Bank. Since the Soviet Union ultimately chose to join neither the IMF nor the World Bank, the United States and its allies and clients have had little trouble dominating both institutions, where voting power is proportional to the quota each nation pays into the institutions. The decisive influence by the United States in the IMF and the World Bank, then, was different from its position in the United Nations, where the Soviet Union had veto power in the Security Council. As a consequence, the U.S. government has preferred to work through the IMF and World Bank, ensuring the Bretton Woods institutions' place as the premier international economic institutions.

But in the decade after World War II, the U.S.-sponsored Marshall Plan eclipsed the World Bank and the IMF in financing the reconstruction of Western Europe. The Marshall Plan, which amounted to around $14 billion (5 percent of GDP in 1948), was a genuine foreign aid program, and through it the United States pumped money into the European economies between 1948 and 1952, along with associated programs for Japan. All together, this first large-scale venture in foreign aid was extremely successful in rebuilding the war-ravaged economies and in inoculating these regions against anticapitalist movements in general and Soviet influence in particular.

The goal of the new institutional framework was stability, and measures that directly attacked an individual nation's payments deficits, such as exchange rate devaluations or tariffs, were to be used only as a last resort and then through orderly, managed, and approved procedures. But there was a significant change in the definition of the problem. As you will recall, both the gold standard and flexible exchange rate systems force adjustments on both deficit and surplus nations as constituent parts of destabilizing payments imbalances. Although it is obvious that there cannot be balance-of-payments deficits without equal balance-of-payments surpluses in the world, the Bretton Woods system singled out deficits as *the* problem at a time that the United States had the largest balance-of-payments surplus in the world. Unlike the gold standard or the flexible exchange rates, the dollar exchange standard placed the burden of adjustment entirely on deficit nations.

The European Economic Community

The fourth important international economic institution in the early post–World War II years was the European Economic Community, first envisioned in 1952. France, Germany, Italy, Belgium, the Netherlands, and Luxembourg, with U.S. support, established the European Steel and Coal Community, a common market in coal, iron ore, steel, and scrap that could be traded among the six signatories without customs or taxes while establishing common tariffs against outside products. One purpose was to increase efficiencies in a sector crucially important for European reconstruction, but there was also a political purpose. France and Germany had long disputed ownership of the coal and iron deposits and steel-making facilities on their common border, and the community was deliberately designed to defuse that continuing tension. The agreement was administered by a High Authority and monitored by supporting institutions that adjudicated disagreements.

The community worked so well that in 1957, the same six nations formed the European Economic Community, a more ambitious effort to create a comprehensive common market that was the second-largest integrated market in the world. The goal was to reduce or eliminate tariffs on all traded goods within the community while maintaining a common external tariff, which, as in the case of Japan, was tolerated by the United States as a part of the reconstruction agenda. In 1971 Ireland, Denmark, and, after considerable British dithering and French resistance, Great Britain joined the European Economic Community. The nine-member community was as large a market as the United States, with 125 percent of the U.S. population.

National agricultural policies posed one of the most problematic initial issues, and they continue to vex members. Each member nation had complex and extensive systems of subsidies to and control of their agricultural sectors, and if there was to be free trade in agricultural products, agricultural policy had to be common through the community. The severe food shortages in Europe during and after World War II gave politicians strong incentives to ensure food security. Moreover, European farmers exercised significant political clout in national, and especially French, politics. After prolonged negotiation, the result was, not surprisingly, the Common Agricultural Policy, which through combinations of price supports, direct income supports, and substantial common agricultural tariffs produced a set of consistent agricultural polices among the community's members.

As soon as European agriculture recovered from World War II, it began to produce surpluses, resembling the U.S. experience with similar programs. These surpluses were stored when possible, exported with the subsidies necessary to sell at world prices, or donated to poor nations, often disrupting national and international agricultural markets.

The Common Agricultural Policy continues to be unpopular with European consumers, who pay high prices, and it was very expensive, accounting for around half of the European Economic Community budget. There were several reform efforts in the 1960s and 1970s, but dissatisfaction with the status quo and reduced political influence by rural constituencies created a strong reform momentum that only began to reshape the entire policy approach in the early 1990s.

Although many U.S. citizens continue to be ambivalent, at best, about dealing with "the other" at home or abroad, much of the structure and operation of the postwar capitalist international and Cold War economy was driven by the United States. Therefore, it is important to understand how the organization and eventual changes of the U.S. economy both reflected and affected the international economy. We begin in the next chapter sketching the key elements of the U.S. domestic economy and politics in the 1950s and into the 1970s, and the conditions by which they functioned successfully.

2

The U.S. Domestic Economy and the International Scene, 1945 to 1970s

The first decades of the twentieth century marked the beginnings of a form of capitalist industrial development organized around mass production and mass consumption. The United States was the leader in this new type of economic dynamism, although similar tendencies were apparent throughout other parts of the industrialized world by the 1950s and 1960s. In this chapter, I describe the ways in which the international economy both reflected and shaped the emergence of U.S. domestic economic institutions and relationships, emphasizing the new forms of economic organization that developed fully in the United States after World War II.

Machine tool and chemical firms were the innovative leaders that transformed the technical conditions of production in some already existing consumer goods, and significant innovations were apparent in the production of entirely new consumer products. Large, machine-using firms became predominant in such traditional products as food processing, cigarettes, soap powders, shoes, spirits, pharmaceuticals, and cosmetics, as well as in new consumer goods like rayon, nylon, plastics, electrical appliances, and the automobile—that ultimate symbol of U.S. consumer civilization. Since both sets of consumer goods were produced with similar capital intensities, large-scale plants, organizations of work, and market organizations, I include both in a single category—modern consumer goods.

Uneven Beginnings

An economy organized around mass production and mass consumption has a distinct logic that required new ways to sustain a workable balance between mass production and mass consumption while reducing the dangers of price wars. This was not an obvious or easy process, and it took several decades until the United States was able to institutionalize the structure appropriate for this new phase of capitalist development. I call this new social formation "Modern Times," the title of Charlie Chaplin's classic 1936 movie about working on an assembly line, and the name evokes the entire era of modernity.

The need for new sets of economic relations and monitoring was obvious in the economic travails of the 1920s, which included erratic profits, less regulation, and increasing concentration in the distribution of income. One of the most serious problems for leading corporations was unrestrained competition, driven in good part by excess productive capacities left over from the stimulus of World War I. Fierce price competition among manufacturing firms selling similar products, between producers and large retailers, and between firms and their suppliers reduced profits, heightened uncertainties, and disrupted the kind of corporate planning essential for the large-scale investments behind mass production.

Business industrial and trade associations tried to eliminate destructive competition by creating orderly markets through the coordination of prices, production, and marketing, working around antitrust legislation. But the efforts failed because of the incentives to cheat and the inability to enforce agreements. State governments' attempts to regulate markets resulted in an ineffective legal patchwork. Constrained by its lack of authority and resources, the federal government in the 1920s did little beyond raising tariffs at the beginning and the end of the decade and establishing a small agricultural price support program in the late 1920s.

Employers and multiple levels of government had successfully suppressed a series of strikes immediately after World War I, and the anticommunist Red Scare created a climate of fear and intimidation in which the U.S. labor movement was on the defensive and divided. A few business leaders began to think beyond their implacable hostility toward labor unions, recognizing that some form of unionization was probably inevitable and that the pummeling of workers and unions had sufficiently weakened and fragmented the labor movement that workers would be receptive to a business-oriented unionism. It was an opportune time to preemptively recognize a few well-behaved unions that would not impinge too seriously on managerial prerogatives.

The incentives for employers were reducing the costliness of breaking strikes and the good chance that a set of politically safe industry-wide unions could perform a useful regulatory function. If unions could establish uniform wages, hours, and work conditions in all firms within a particular product line, they would remove one of the foremost sources of differential production costs that encouraged price competition. Moreover, as long as higher wages did not severely disadvantage important fractions of capital, greater working-class purchasing power was beneficial in expanding mass markets.

As employers mulled over such a change in strategy, they were a part of a major transformation in corporate governance: the people making such suggestions and even decisions were not always the corporations' owners. The nineteenth-century entrepreneurial heroes/robber barons of mid- to late nineteenth-century capitalism such as Cornelius Vanderbilt (shipping and railroads), John D. Rockefeller (petroleum refining), Andrew Carnegie (steel), J. P. Morgan (finance), and Marshall Field (department stores) were directly involved in running their firms, but a fundamental shift was becoming evident. As the nineteenth century turned into the twentieth, the role of professional managers increased in day-to-day operations, and the role of owners (stock holders, represented by boards of directors) in operational decisions receded. While a board of directors was supposed to supervise management, increasingly even large stock holders came to regard their holdings as one component of their financial portfolios, and their interest in actually running the business was slight, as long as stock price and dividends were satisfactory. On the other side of things, the complexity of these giant organizations did require a range of expertise that educational institutions were beginning to include in their curricula, and the graduates were not enthusiastic about meddling or even scrutiny by amateurs, rich or not. The effect was the beginning of the separation of corporate control from corporate ownership, a tendency that continued to grow through the twentieth century.

A spectacular stock market bubble in the late 1920s doubled the Dow Jones industrial stock index in eighteen months, and its collapse in 1929 preceded the onset of the Great Depression of the 1930s. This drama undercut any strategies for dampening cutthroat competition and creating a successful economic organization appropriate for mass production and mass consumption. The abrupt 50 percent decline of international commerce, the fragility of domestic financial systems, and the inability to match levels of mass consumption with the levels of mass production in a chaotically changing economic landscape all converged to create the most serious capitalist crisis ever. Between 1929 and 1934, U.S. production declined by a third and official unemployment rates rose to over 25 percent of the nonfarm workforce, but even so, U.S. political decentralization, capitalists' disarray, and the belief in the healing power of deflation obstructed an effective political response.

The administration of President Franklin Delano Roosevelt, inaugurated in 1933, initiated a number of experimental policies, collectively known as the New Deal. The short-lived National Industrial Recovery Act of 1933 was an attempt at national industrial planning by the New Deal, backing up with federal law what industrial business and trade associations had tried in the 1920s. Even though business leaders dominated the councils empowered to make decisions about prices, wages, and output levels, the NIRA's failure to bring order into markets soon turned the business community's support into opposition. In any case, the U.S. Supreme Court ruled it unconstitutional in 1935.

Other policies enjoyed greater success. The National Labor Relations Act (1935) legalized (and regulated) union organization. The Glass-Steagall Act (1933), passed in response to massive bank failures and forced mergers in the early years of the Great Depression, established deposit insurance, gave new regulatory powers to the Federal Reserve System, and defined specific financial activities, and only those activities, as appropriate for brokerage houses, insurance companies, and different types of banks. The Social Security Act (1935) mandated a national pension system and some limited social insurance, although by excluding agricultural and domestic service workers, it neglected large numbers of poor, minority, women, and middle-aged workers, who received only token benefits after retirement. Federal health insurance was not envisioned.

These acts had some support among some business leaders, but in any case, the Depression had undermined the hold of business ideology and increased the power of the federal government, which in turn strengthened labor unions and popular electoral power. The entire New Deal endeavor has to be understood as an effort to put the business system back on its feet, even while it had to overcome opposition by the business community to do so.

Roosevelt's New Deal also included a myriad of more focused initiatives, ranging from agricultural price supports, the Civilian Conservation Corps, the Work Projects Administration, and other regulatory, public works, and relief initiatives. Nevertheless, when Hitler's army invaded the Polish Corridor in late 1939, the U.S. unemployment rate of the nonfarm workforce was still 17 percent.

World War II rescued U.S. capitalism from the Depression. Business opposition to wartime federal regulation and control all but evaporated as soon as large federal expenditures for war materiel raised profit prospects and unions agreed to a no-strike pledge. During the war, the federal government successfully operated a regime of war capitalism that went far beyond New Deal legislation in its comprehensiveness, tight controls, top-down commands, and rationing of food and fuel. These wartime controls and management created full employment, new occupational opportunities for women, modest improvements in the distribution of income, and new possibilities of civil rights for African Americans.

The federal government dismantled the mechanisms of direct governmental economic management soon after the war, but the Employment Act of 1946 formally obligated the federal government to ensure full employment by managing effective demand through fiscal and monetary policies mapped out by John Maynard Keynes' pathbreaking book *The General Theory of Employment, Interest, and Money* (1936). This was followed closely by the Taft-Hartley Act of 1947, which constrained the freedoms that the Wagner Act had accorded organized labor, strengthened conservative union leaders' control over members, and mandated purging unions of left-wing troublemakers. The Taft-Hartley Act was a direct response to the wave of postwar strikes set off by the rank-and-file membership despite opposition by union leaders, and to employers' fears that the Employment Act would strengthen labor's bargaining position.

As I argued in the first chapter, the debacle of the Great Depression and success of wartime regulations and controls convinced significant portions of U.S. political and economic leadership that an unregulated market could be dangerous to capitalism and that government controls could stabilize the economy and sustain profits. Substantial federal economic involvement and regulation (the mixed economy) characterized the postwar decades. Some parts of the necessary institutional and policy structure were deliberately created, others emerged in a more serendipitous fashion, and a range of other, complementary social reorderings supported it.

One of the key social reorderings of the Modern Times social formation was to enable large swaths of the unionized working class to achieve a family wage—a wage sufficiently high to make financially feasible having only one member of a family employed. This was a longtime aspiration of male members of labor unions, and it encouraged an ideology that idealized the nuclear family with father as the breadwinner and mother as the homemaker. While the extent to which this family ideology was reflected in reality is doubtful, historical misconstructions about the 1950s family continue to enjoy considerable political salience. Those myths, however, contain a profound irony for those who laud the *Leave It to Beaver/Father Knows Best/Brady Bunch* model of white middle-class families. If such family life did exist in statistically significant numbers, it was this family model that by the 1960s and 1970s had produced the white middle-class political radicals, counterculture young adults, and many of the African American civil rights leaders.

The construction and operation of the postwar Modern Times model was made possible by a unique and stringent condition: the United States was the preeminent industrial producer of the world. This industrial dominance was complemented by its military power, including an initial monopoly on atomic weapons. The U.S. preeminence in manufacturing was yoked to a new political will to assert that preeminence in the international realm. In addition, the lack of significant foreign competition in domestic markets enabled the United States to avoid a conflict between promoting unrestricted international trade and investment and preserving and expanding a modest domestic system of national welfare capitalism.

The Structure of Modern Times in the 1950s and 1960s

Some basic economic relationships and their links to the international economy illustrate the significance of the Modern Times model. Industrial capitalism has certainly changed in significant ways over the last two hundred and fifty or so years, but there are two basic, enduring features that are integral to its very definition as a mode of production. The first is the wage-labor system, with the resulting conflict between propertyless workers, who have only their labor services to sell, and the propertied classes and their agents who purchase labor services. This is the capital-labor relationship.

The second feature of industrial capitalism is profit-motivated production by private firms that compete with each other in product markets to realize profits. The capital-labor struggle and the interfirm relationships (capital-capital competition) are the two principal driving forces of capitalism, and they are set in national political frameworks with shifting Public Sector–citizen relationships. These three sets of social and political relations underlie the principal sectors of the Modern Times social and economic order.

In presenting the central elements and interrelationships of Modern Times, I employ a stylized version of it by adapting the three sectors into which James O'Connor in *The Fiscal Crisis of the State* (2001) divided the economy, here naming the sectors Core, Competitive, and Public. While it is difficult to draw precise lines among sectors, the general contours are reasonably clear.

The Core Sector

After World War II, there was a stable set of highly profitable U.S. manufacturing corporations with sophisticated, capital-intensive production technologies. These corporations had developed systems of work divided and supervised along the principles of scientific management—work tasks broken in minute components for easier surveillance, unionized labor forces, and rising labor productivity. These corporations were important members of the Core Sector, and corporations producing modern consumer goods—standardized consumer durables (automobiles, electrical appliances, and so on) and mass-produced nondurable consumer goods (pharmaceuticals, cos-

metics, detergents, cigarettes, processed foods, for example)—
composed its dynamic center. Firms that produced intermediate
and capital goods, such as steel and other metals, fuel, power,
plastics, glass, chemicals, and machinery, sold most of their output to modern consumer goods producers and were also in the
Core Sector. Finally, many firms supplied a range of services for
Core Sector firms, such as finance, insurance, communications,
transportation, and marketing, and they also are usefully considered to be part of the sector.

In regards to the capital-capital relationship in the Core
Sector, the firms' market organization compelled the few large
corporations that dominated each market—oligopolies, in the
parlance of economics—to engage in co-respective nonprice
competition through advertising, product differentiation, and
distribution and product services. As demonstrated in the 1920s,
price competition was risky, because it could easily degenerate
into price wars from which customers benefited and firms lost.
The lack of aggressive price competition among large corporations became so evident in the 1950s and 1960s that the professional economics literature contained frequent contentions that
corporate managers had opted to achieve an easy life rather than
aggressively pursue profit maximizing.

In the absence of foreign competition and with wages a
smaller proportion of total cost than in smaller enterprises, Core
firms' market power made it in their interests to strike an im-
plicit bargain with unions: high wages and benefits in exchange
for control over the organization of work. A wage increase, felt
throughout an industry through industry-wide unions, would
signal all three or four or five major producers to exert their market power and recover the higher labor costs by raising product
prices. Moreover, increased wages across the Core Sector were
capable of stimulating Core workers' demand for Core products
and reducing excess capacity, thus lowering average fixed costs
and increasing profits despite higher labor costs.

In general, Core firms' market power enabled them to
capture and retain the fruits of cost reductions within the
enterprises, whether the cost reductions stemmed from labor

productivity, technical or organizational innovation, or materials prices. These increased earnings were then distributed, albeit not evenly, among corporate employees and owners, and here the struggle occasionally turned nasty. Nevertheless, the struggles were set within narrow parameters: wages, benefits, hours, working conditions, seniority rights; that is, the division of corporate revenues. Decisions about choice of what was to be produced and how it was going to be made were not on the table.

The market structure of Modern Times thus prevented the benefits of productivity increases in the Core Sector from being diffused widely throughout the economy and society by means of lower product prices, and this sharply curtailed the trickledown effect expected by competitive market theory. Above-market remuneration meant that more people were willing to work at the Core Sector's relatively desirable administrative and production jobs than the number of positions available. Once obtained, the jobs could become lifelong careers in the firm. With the exception of clerical work and the occasional director of personnel, production and administrative positions were monopolized by men.

Core Sector production workers' new position in the middle ranks of income receivers encouraged these men and many of their family members to identify themselves as consumers and taxpayers rather than as workers. This tendency was reinforced by their financial stake in current arrangements through home ownership, the real value of which generally rose, and a piece of union pension funds that became important players in financial markets.

The Competitive Sector

The Core Sector was the distinguishing feature of Modern Times and the dominant force in the economy, but it was not the only way in which commodity production was organized. Most U.S. employees worked in quite different settings: small, low-profit, and low-wage enterprises with high failure rates. They operated in competitive product markets with little or no market power, and this capital-capital relationship governed their capital-labor relations. Competitive Sector firms were labor intensive, employed the majority of minority and women workers, and experienced high turnovers of employees. These enterprises, many using both wage and family labor, included small factories, laundries, artisanal enterprises, retail stores, restaurants, small farms, and a wide range of services in both formal and informal work situations. The scale, structure, and instability of work in the Competitive Sector were as severe an obstacle as employer resistance to organizing effective labor unions.

Not everyone in the Competitive Sector was poor. Many independent professionals, such as physicians, lawyers, morticians, accountants, and financial advisers, made comfortable livings and bought modern consumer goods. Some employers who operated in genuinely competitive markets and a range of tradespeople, such as electricians, plumbers, machinists, and surveyors, also did well materially in the Competitive Sector. In both the professions and the trades, those in occupations in which government-enforced certification and licensing requirements limited new entrants were particularly likely to flourish.

Modern Times agriculture and retailing illustrate the highly complex and heterogeneous nature of the Competitive Sector. Some food processing and the production of agricultural inputs (machinery, fuels, fertilizers, herbicides, and insecticides) were securely Core Sector activities, and Core-type production processes (factories in the field) became important in chicken and lettuce production. The competitiveness of agricultural product markets, however, prevented agricultural capital from controlling its markets and from constructing Core-type accords with labor. But agricultural capital did wield considerable political clout to ensure government price supports, production quotas, tariffs, and subsidized research and credit as well as the seasonal immigration of Mexican *bra-ceros*. These policies helped significant fractions of agricultural capital to reap incomes more like those of Core capital while agricultural labor and food processing workers in meat and chicken packing worked and lived under Competitive Sector conditions.

Several retail service firms began to apply Core organizational forms and created a series of successful hybrid enterprises. In corporate size, profits, and work organization, McDonald's fast-food chain was clearly Core, but in other key features—labor intensity, general work conditions (such as pay and job stability), and therefore the composition of its labor force—it more closely resembled the Competitive Sector. Other large firms in direct retail sales, such as Sears & Roebuck, J.C. Penney's, and Montgomery Ward's, including their catalogue business dependent on telephone and mail order, had similar hybrid characteristics. In the 1960s, Kmart, Target, and Wal-mart opened their first stores and launched the era of big-box discount retailers, and they had similar hybrid characteristics. These mixed features predicted a new set of economic arrangements that was to develop more fully in the late twentieth and early twenty-first centuries.

The Public Sector

The differential patterns of the Core and Competitive Sectors' development generated divergent tendencies. In the Core Sector, wages rose, but there were relatively few new employment opportunities. On the other hand, while wage rates in the Competitive Sector could rise, they also had downward flexibility, because the sector responded to variations in total demand and absorbed workers unable to find more desirable employment. Since the structure impeded significant trickle-down effects, economic growth could produce prosperity, security, and hope at one end of the spectrum and poverty, insecurity, and despair at the other.

The Public Sector implemented policies to deal with the centrifugal forces of Modern Times in a number of ways. While most of the Public Sector's activities were not directly productive in the conventional market sense, all three levels of government were major employers. Supported by rising unionization and the explicit use of parity principles regarding wages, salaries, and work conditions, Public Sector jobs were linked with those in the Core Sector, and relatively desirable Public Sector employment, again like that in the Core, was restricted primarily by the availability of positions. Public employment was an important tool in dampening dissent from the unemployed and underpaid, but the Public Sector's major role in sustaining the Modern Times system was through different avenues of expenditure policy, most notably at the federal level.

Large portions of the federal government's direct purchases were for armaments (a.k.a. defense), justified by the Cold War and occasional hot wars, and they shaded over to another, more general public expenditure purpose of stabilizing effective demand for corporate products through Keynesian-style demand management. Armament expenditures to keep the United States and its allies and clients safe from anticapitalist movements, all labeled communist no matter their nature, made it politically feasible to engage in large federal expenditures that increased effective demand for goods and services. These massive federal expenditures were politically palatable because they did not compete with significant private interests at either the local or national level.

The second principal function of government expenditure policy was to foster political acceptance of current arrangements by reducing or suppressing disaffection and political unrest. Vigorous employment growth was helpful in this regard, but special provisions had to be made for those who benefited slightly or not at all from the weak Modern Times trickle-down effects. In the 1950s and 1960s, the federal and state governments directly allocated some resources for safety-net programs, such as Aid to Families with Dependent Children (1935, expanded 50 percent during the 1960s and early 1970s), the Food Stamp Act (1964), Job Corps (1964), Head Start (1965), Medicaid (1965), and Medicare (1965), and expanded unemployment benefits to alleviate the material hardship of those in (or fallen out of) the Competitive Sector as well as targeting children and older citizens. Most of these policies were parts of President Lyndon Johnson's War on Poverty that lost momentum with the 1968 election of President Richard M. Nixon. Many social policies of this sort were supported by liberal corporations—Core Sector firms that, as with wage increases, could pass on higher taxes through raising their product prices.

The extent and depth of social policies were limited by the Cold War, which exerted a strong social control role. Any domestic political initiative that threatened to redistribute power or more than a small amount of income could be labeled socialist or communist and successfully defined as like the enemy—illegitimate, un-American, and traitorous. In this way, Cold War fears effectively enforced strict limits on welfare capitalism and social democratic possibilities.

The government sponsorship of Core Sector profitability kept significant fragments of capital supporting an active public sector. Modern Times structures and the federal government strengthened unionized workers' influence in national politics, and the more even political balance between labor and capital, along with the expansion of agreed-upon government functions, enabled the government apparatus itself to exercise a more independent influence.

The Cold War and the Development Project

At the end of World War I, the United States had pressured the Allies to pay their debts, and the Allies imposed heavy reparation payments on Germany. Both moves proved to be mistakes, and the United States took the opposite tack in the decade after World War II. The United States canceled much of the Allies' public debts and sponsored the Marshall Plan for Europe and similar programs for Japan that were the first large-scale ventures in foreign aid. These efforts were successful in enabling both Allies and previous enemies to recover economically. Germany and Japan recovered so rapidly because both already were modern industrialized societies, and their need was principally to repair and reconstruct physical plants, equipment, and infrastructure. The very success of this effort, including reorienting the economies toward mass production and mass consumption, meant that both soon became formidable competitors in the international economy.

Despite successes in Western Europe and Japan, U.S. policymakers in the late 1940s and early 1950s were deeply disturbed by the turbulence and shifts in political power in the rest of the world: the convulsions of independence and partition of India and Pakistan (1947); the Berlin blockade (1948); the creation of Israel in Palestine (1948); the triumph of the communist revolution in China (1949); the Soviet Union's detonation of an atom bomb (1949); bitter anticolonial struggles in Greece, Malaya (now Malaysia), Indonesia, Vietnam, and Algeria; the Korean War (1950–1953); growing resistance to colonial rule throughout the rest of Africa, Asia, and the Caribbean; and the penchant for reformers to win democratic elections in settings as disparate as Guatemala and Iran (both "corrected" by U.S.-engineered coups in 1954). U.S. officials feared a world spinning out of control and were compelled to pay more attention to Africa, Asia, and Latin America to offset Soviet inroads. With the triumph of the Chinese revolution, the Cold War broadened to a truly global scale.

Along with the military dimensions of the Cold War, the U.S. government launched programs to encourage economic development in Africa, Asia, and Latin America—the so-called Third World. President Harry Truman, in his 1949 Point Four doctrine, formally announced the intention of the U.S. government to promote poor nations' economic growth and to alleviate worldwide poverty and misery—conditions that were considered "breeding grounds for communism."

The Birth of the Third World

The 1954 Bandung conference of unaligned Asian and African nations adopted the term *Third World* for the societies that were aspiring to industrialization and prosperity. Many of these nations had recently become independent of European colonial empires or were struggling to do so, and they rejected the tutelage of either the industrialized capitalist First World or the communist Second World. The Third World category always included an extremely heterogeneous bunch of places, and the differences among the Third World nations have increased rapidly in the last few decades of the twentieth century. The oil-rich nations of the Middle East and the "Newly Industrialized Countries" (NICs, such as South Korea, Taiwan, Brazil, and Mexico) experienced substantial material progress, and others, such as the countries of sub-Saharan Africa, became even poorer. Moreover, the dissolution of the Soviet Union in the early 1990s meant that an identifiable Second World has been replaced by so-called economies in transition (to market capitalism). These problems with the Third World designation have led some observers to favor the use of "South" versus "North," a representation with its own difficulties (what about Australia, New Zealand, South Africa?). I recognize the problems of any shorthand term, but convenience demands something, and I have chosen Third World for its historical and descriptive power. I use a variety of terms for the industrialized, prosperous nations, such as metropolitan countries, rich countries, and others.

The consequent development program underwrote an elaborate and extensively interlocked development establishment of U.S. government agencies, universities, and foundations, international institutions, and some foreign agencies, all of which dispensed and monitored foreign aid and loans, expert advice, and sponsored research. The principal intellectual paradigms that informed U.S. thought about economic development framed the issues in terms of "poor nations" and "rich nations" rather than of poor peoples and rich peoples, thus avoiding uncomfortable questions about class disparities at home and abroad.

U.S. rhetorical support for industrial development was in line with the nationalist ambitions of Third World leaders, including those in newly decolonized and politically independent states. Four years after the end of World War II, the United Nations Economic Commission for Latin America issued a report that recommended import-substituting industrialization policies to stimulate Latin American industrial development. The report elevated and formalized import-substituting industrialization—the ad hoc defensive package of tariffs, currency controls, and subsidies used by governments of the more urbanized and industrialized Third World nations to survive the crisis of the Great Depression. The UN policy recommendations echoed the early nineteenth-century arguments of Alexander Hamilton of the United States and Friedrich List in Germany, and the postwar import-substituting model was very similar to the policies used by the U.S. and German governments to spur their exceptional industrial development in the late nineteenth and early twentieth centuries.

The reasoning behind the UN Economic Commission recommendations was that the export of primary products had failed to generate the industrial development necessary to raise the material welfare of Third World nations and that disadvantageous price movements between primary and secondary products would ensure that the strategy would continue to fail. The report argued that the proper role of primary-product exports was to finance the imports necessary for urban and industrial development, and the foreign trade sector had to be deliberately managed for this to occur.

The Economic Commission's report, like almost all United Nations reports, assiduously avoided political commentary. Nevertheless, the political weakening of Third World elites based on primary-product exports during the Depression and the concomitant strengthening of urban-industrial interests, including the political incorporation of labor unions, made such development policies politically feasible. Third World leaders in Latin America and the new nations of Africa and Asia almost universally adopted the model of tapping primary-product exports to finance domestic urban and domestic industrial growth behind tariff walls. India went beyond the import-substituting policy package and drew more from Soviet practices, including diluted Five-Year Plans and a more direct, command-economy approach in directing new investment and restricting foreign firms than was practiced in Latin America.

The New Transnational Corporation

In the post–World War II period, U.S. foreign direct investment not only surpassed U.S. foreign portfolio investment, it became larger by a factor of four. In 1938, U.S. foreign direct investment in Third World nations, typically in mines, oil wells, plantations, ranches, forestry, and the occasional urban utility, was two-thirds of total U.S. foreign direct investment. Foreign direct investment in Latin America was three times the level of U.S. foreign direct investment in Europe. By the early 1970s, however, U.S. foreign direct investment in Japan and Europe was three times the U.S. foreign direct investment in Latin America.

These geographical shifts are explained by sectoral shifts: the predominant form of postwar U.S. foreign direct investment was to create the capacity to manufacture modern consumer goods abroad to sell in those foreign markets. That is, a U.S. manufacturer invested (built a plant) in Indonesia and made automobiles (or electrical appliances, pharmaceuticals, cosmetics, breakfast cereal, and so on) in Indonesia to sell to Indonesians. This type of investment contrasted sharply with industrialized nations' earlier foreign direct investment in Third World nations, which was dominated by investments abroad in the production and transportation of resource-based products for the markets of their own and other industrialized nations. This is what was new about the new transnational corporation.

U.S.-based transnational corporations expanded rapidly during the 1950s and 1960s, and in the mid-1970s, half of world transnational corporation investment was still from the United

States, although that proportion was declining. By 1971 foreign production of U.S. transnational corporations was almost four times the value of U.S. exports, and between 1957 and 1974 the proportion of total U.S. corporate profits from overseas operations rose from 8.6 percent to 26.9 percent. Transnational corporations were almost exclusively Core Sector firms, and of the nine largest manufacturing firms in the United States for which data are available, profits derived from foreign operations averaged well over 50 percent of total profits.

This change in the character of U.S. foreign direct investment from primary to secondary sectors derived from the competitive structure of the U.S. Modern Times economy. The avoidance of price competition inhibited increasing market share for individual firms, and another strategy was needed to expand sales. Export markets were a possible avenue for sales expansion, but there were trade barriers, and exports still raised the specter of potential price wars with other large U.S. firms. Diversification into other product lines through the conglomerate movement was one frequently traveled avenue around these limitations, and another was becoming a transnational corporation.

By establishing production operations in a foreign site, U.S. producers could expand sales without disrupting market arrangements within the United States, neutralize other competition, and exercise significant market power in foreign venues. Modern Times transnational corporations were not seeking cheap labor, nor were they looking for resource-based export possibilities; they sought actual and potential markets for modern consumer goods by establishing production facilities in those markets.

Transnational corporations were quite selective about the choice of location. What the transnational corporations wanted, first of all, was a stable and promising domestic market. This criterion meant that transnational corporations were attracted to places such as Canada, Australia, and Europe that were generally prosperous, or to countries like Brazil, India, and South Africa that were less prosperous but had affluent minorities that could be substantial markets for modern consumer goods. On the negative side, post–World War II uncertainties and instabilities in the recently independent nations of Africa and Southeast Asia discouraged transnational corporations, and of course, they were not welcome in communist countries at this time. Finally, India and the fastest growing East Asian economies could have been desirable locations, but their closely regulated domestic markets restricted transnational corporations' freedom of action.

In another part of the world, the European Economic Community had a common tariff around the six member nations, and Third World nations' frequent adoption of import-substituting industrialization policies impeded exporting to them. The difficulties of penetrating those markets from the outside raised the incentives for transnational corporation direct investment. A corollary of this point is that if a transnational corporation located production facilities in one European or Latin American nation, its products often had easy access to several other nations' markets through common market arrangements. The EEC was by far the most successful and developed common market, but common markets in the 1960s and 1970s had become popular, especially in Latin America, as a way to increase the size of domestic markets without redistributing income. In these decades, the Latin American Free Trade Area, the Central American Common Market, and the Andean Pact offered the advantages of multination access to markets by transnational corporations, and there were a number of experiments on other continents.

The bulk of foreign direct investment by U.S. transnational corporations was in Europe, but the change in the sectoral composition of foreign direct investment was particularly striking in Latin America, where foreign investors had traditionally favored mineral and agricultural products by wide margins. The shift in U.S. direct investment toward manufacturing profoundly altered foreign firms' interests in local politics. The United Fruit Company, Anaconda Copper, and Standard Oil are examples of the older pattern. These firms historically produced resource-based exports in Latin America for industrialized nations' markets, and their interests in the host nations were extremely narrow.

Beyond certain fundamental needs—access to resources, a supportive business environment, unproblematic labor relations, low taxes, and free movement of corporate goods, personnel, and profits—resource-oriented foreign investors had little in the way of other interests in whatever nation was involved. By contrast, foreign investors like General Electric, Chevrolet, Volkswagen, General Foods, Bayer, and Procter & Gamble that were selling in the markets of their foreign host, had a direct stake in expanding local markets for their products. For the old-style foreign investor oriented toward resource-based exports, vigorous domestic economic growth would have caused unwanted complications and probably raised the cost of doing business. Modern Times transnational corporations, on the other hand, became supporters of national economic development as long as they were in a position to profit from domestic economic growth.

The publicly sponsored development project, a product of the Cold War, involved active promotion of economic reform and stimulation in Third World nations, an effort that expanded local markets for modern consumer goods and therefore was congruent with the newly situated interests of U.S. capital in its transnational corporations. But the reformist and developmental impulse of U.S. government officials and transnational corporations was not robust, because the development project, if it worked, too often produced a politics unacceptable to transnational corporations and the U.S. government. For example, the International Telephone and Telegraph Company (now ITT Corporation) was and is a highly diversified manufacturing and communications U.S. transnational corporation. In 1973 it worked closely with the Chilean military to overthrow and assassinate democratically elected President Salvador Allende of Chile, leader of the Socialist Party. The brutal military dictatorship lasted almost twenty years, and the entire process demonstrates that new forms of transnational corporations could behave in a traditional manner. As a result of increasing Third World political conflicts and instability, the U.S. government soon subordinated its reform and development efforts to counterinsurgency, suppression of popular movements, and the formation of national security states.

This sketch of Modern Times has emphasized the manner in which the formation worked and has virtually ignored the ways in which it did not work. As a consequence, I have obscured the frictions, contradictions, and ephemeral nature of the conditions necessary for the functioning of what some scholars, in retrospect, have called the Golden Age of Capitalism. This perspective is in line with the optimism of those times, when pluralism in political science, structural functionalism in sociology, and Keynesianism in economics reigned supreme. This was a confidence that assured people that academic technicians understood the highly complex character of national and international problems and that they would solve them as soon as they could overcome the irrational or narrowly self-serving resistance by the benighted. Existing inequities and injustices within the United States and the ugly, disastrous war in Southeast Asia appeared capable of being remedied by technical competence, better policy, goodwill, and continuing economic growth. By the 1970s, however, the foundations of Modern Times began to come apart at the seams, exposing the underlying economic and political frailties of what had seemed to be a robust and progressive social formation.

3

U.S. Political Shifts and beyond Bretton Woods, 1970s to 1980s

U.S. world dominance in manufacturing was a necessary condition for the smooth functioning of the U.S. domestic economic arrangements that I have called Modern Times in the United States. But the very success of the Bretton Woods framework created forces that eventually undermined the post–World War II international system. Nevertheless, the buoyancy of the international economy contributed to U.S. prosperity in the 1950s and 1960s and made possible some new social policies as well as contributed to some major changes in the parameters of U.S. politics, changes more durable than the Bretton Woods agreement.

Bretton Woods Success

In its own terms, the Bretton Woods system definitely succeeded. Average tariffs on manufactured goods declined sharply, foreign trade and investment grew rapidly, and exchange rates and the international economy as a whole achieved a decent level of stability.

The most-favored-nation clause of the General Agreement on Tariffs and Trade stipulated that when two countries negotiated tariff reductions between themselves, they were obligated to extend those terms to all signatory nations. This clause was a subset of a more general principle against discriminating against any member nation. By the 1960s, European and U.S. nonagricultural tariffs had declined by a third or a half, depending on who was doing the measuring. But these tariff reductions did little to open industrial nations' markets to Third World exports, which tended to be unprocessed agricultural and mineral products.

Fewer trade restrictions and international financial stability enabled a rapid expansion of international trade and investment that in turn contributed to postwar prosperity. The value of world exports in constant prices (the "real" value) between 1950 and 1973 rose an average of almost 8 percent a year, generating a total increase of four and five times. East Asian nations' export growth was the greatest, but European exporters also did well, with average export growth often into the double digits. U.S. exports rose at the more modest rate of 6.3 percent annually, and by 1973 the annual value of U.S. exports had fallen to second place, behind Germany.

Between 1950 and 1973, the growth of exports was 60 percent greater than that of world gross domestic product (GDP), and the proportion of total exports to world GDP rose from 7 percent in 1950 to over 11 percent by 1973. Exports as a proportion of each nation's GDP rose for most countries, some doubling or tripling, while the U.S. proportion rose less dramatically from 3 percent to 5 percent of GDP. In sharp contrast to this general trend, the export-GDP proportions declined in Latin America and India, demonstrating the effect of import-substituting industrialization policies. Foreign investment also rose, and as noted in previous chapters, U.S. foreign direct investment in new transnational corporations surged until it was four times the value of foreign portfolio investment.

Two decades of growing U.S. affluence, albeit with cyclical interruptions, were buttressed by the dynamic international economy. While the Cold War and the Korean and Vietnam wars stained the era and strained the nation economically and politically, overriding confidence and optimism underlay major political initiatives that in turn altered U.S. politics.

Political Changes in the United States

The first major change was the civil rights movement that built on a century of African American struggles against Jim Crow laws in the South and extralegal racial discrimination in the North. The second change was the women's rights movement that also built on a century of agitation and politicking by women for more opportunities in education, careers, and health care.

The 1954 Supreme Court opinion in *Brown v. Board of Education* (Topeka, Kansas) that declared racial segregation in public schools to be a violation of the U.S. Constitution was a major national-level victory for the civil rights movement. There were several federal legislative steps from there, and the principal watersheds were the Civil Rights Act of 1964, initiated by President John F. Kennedy and pushed through by President Lyndon B. Johnson after Kennedy's assassination, and the Voting Rights Act of 1965. The Civil Rights Act went beyond race, the principal focus, and contained a prohibition of discrimination on the basis of "sex" (gender) by employers, inserted by an ardent segregationist senator from Virginia who voted against the Act.

The young white middle-class political activists who grew up in the 1950s were important supporters of the civil rights and women's movements, although some political energy was drawn off by anti–Vietnam War and antidraft struggles. On the other side, white Southern politicians bitterly fought racial desegregation, and the Southern senators' filibuster ended only when enforcement provisions were diluted. "States' rights"—evoking the Confederacy—was the language used by opponents used to justify their position. The passage of the 1964 act both acknowledged and moved to reduce a major source of embarrassment for the United States in the international community, since U.S. treatment of African Americans violated the U.S. Constitution and the United Nations 1948 Declaration of Human Rights.

White Southern politicians' dislike and fear of federal attempts to provide civil rights protections, and to a lesser degree women's rights, made them ripe for seceding from the Democratic Party. An early move in that direction was the short-lived States' Rights Democratic Party ("Dixicrats"), created to support of the 1948 presidential campaign by former South Carolina governor and future U.S. senator Strom Thurmond. This campaign was in the wake of President Harry S. Truman's 1948 executive order prohibiting racial segregation and discrimination in the U.S. military. The new party had little effect on the election and soon disappeared.

When Richard Nixon, President Dwight D. Eisenhower's former vice president, campaigned the second time for president in 1968, he and his circle of advisers decided that white segregationist Democrats in the South would be vulnerable to a Republican appeal based on race, coded to varying degrees, along with an explicit anticommunism. This "southern strategy" was tricky; after all, many Republicans at that time still proudly proclaimed themselves to be of the "party of Lincoln"; Republican President Eisenhower sent U.S. Army troops into Arkansas to integrate Little Rock Central High School in 1957. The southern strategy was further complicated by Alabama governor George C. Wallace's segregationist third-party candidacy.

Wallace won in five Southern states, but by 1972 the Southern strategy was beginning to work. Although the Watergate scandal forced President Nixon's resignation in 1974, elected white officials in the South were switching from the Democratic Party to the Republican Party, and new candidates for elected office increasingly opted for the Republican label. Southern states were again one-party states, although a different party. White Southerners—barely a quarter of the U.S. population—have been much more successful in putting their sectional stamp on U.S. policies through the Republican Party than through the Democratic Party or third parties.[1]

President Nixon's legacy in international affairs is substantial. He relaxed the embargo on trade with China in 1971, initiated U.S. diplomatic recognition of China, negotiated the 1972 treaty with the Soviet Union to limit nuclear arms, and withdrew the U.S. military from Vietnam in 1973. This is an impressive list, but President Nixon's role in ending the Bretton Woods framework probably had a greater impact around the world than any of his other foreign policy decisions.

International Competition and the Collapse of the Dollar Exchange Standard

An alternative to import-substituting policies for Third World economic development emerged in the mid-1960s. Instead of depending on the protection of domestic markets from competition from imports to develop manufacturing, German and Japanese manufacturing firms in the immediate post–World War II years, jump-started by U.S. aid, rebuilt using newer and more efficient production processes often developed in the United States but ahead of what many U.S. firms were willing to finance and install. While still protecting domestic markets, Germans began using manufactured exports as a platform for general economic expansion, reflecting Germany's experience in the world economy in the late nineteenth and early twentieth centuries. The Japanese also began to orient their industry to foreign markets, beginning with inexpensive, simple manufactured items of uneven quality. Guided, subsidized, and generally encouraged by government policy, Japanese industries quickly moved up the ladders of product quality and complexity, and by the end of the 1960s, Honda, Toyota, Sony, and other Japanese brands were becoming respected and desired throughout the world.

Both reconstructed economies successfully employed governmentally approved and supported development strategies based on manufactured exports, which unlike primary-product exports stimulated other domestic manufacturing, which remained protected from foreign competition by trade barriers. After initially employing import-substituting industrialization policies, the authoritarian governments of South Korea and Taiwan (a.k.a. "Nationalist China" as opposed to "Communist China" after 1949) as well as the semi-city-states of Singapore and Hong Kong, which possessed few primary products to export but many skilled workers, began encouraging industrial exports as a platform for general economic development. As in the case of Germany and Japan, they were aided in this project by receiving millions upon millions in U.S. aid and privileged access to U.S. markets because of their status as frontline nations in the Cold War. They were remarkably successful in creating dynamic export manufacturing sectors, quickly moving into new, more complex products with higher markups, working up from textiles and stuffed animals to steel to electronics and, in the case of South Korea, shipbuilding.

Germany, Japan, and subsequently South Korea, Taiwan, Singapore, and Hong Kong rapidly became formidable competitors in international markets of manufactured products. The foreign penetration of foreign and domestic markets for U.S. manufacturing firms began in the 1960s and, once started, increased quickly. U.S. imports of goods and services were less than 4 percent of GDP in the late 1940s, and while the proportion grew slowly through the next two decades, it rose sharply during the 1970s and 1980s; imports equaled 12.7 percent of GDP by 1989 (and 17.6 percent by 2008). As a consequence of weakening international markets for U.S. manufactured goods, agricultural exports constituted larger shares of total U.S. exports in the late 1970s and 1980s.

One possible response by U.S. firms to foreign competition would have been to raise trade barriers against foreign products. The protectionist impulse in the United States was by no means dead, but the U.S. business community was deeply divided on this issue. For example, in the U.S. auto industry during the 1970s and 1980s, General Motors owned Saab and Opel and had acquired large stakes in Isuzu, Suzuki, Fiat, and Subaru. Ford Motor Company owned Jaguar, Volvo, Land

Rover, and a large interest in Mazda. Chrysler became little more than an operating division of DaimlerChrysler, which owned a third of the Mitsubishi auto company. With this kind of interpenetration, the idea of protecting the U.S. market from foreign automobile manufacturers had lost much of its clarity. In addition, many foreign companies followed the U.S. example by engaging in foreign direct investment into the United States to open auto and other manufacturing plants in the United States. These so-called transplants further complicated the design of protectionist legislation.

The U.S. government was further handicapped in an effort to protect domestic markets by already low barriers against imported manufactures and by its postwar record of pushing for freer multilateral international trade in manufactures—both legacies of the time when U.S. manufacturers had little international competition. Even so, there was good old arm-twisting. A series of informal "voluntary" quotas ("Gentlemen's Agreements" and "Orderly Market Agreements") slowed the imports of foreign automobiles and textiles into the United States for a time.

The new international competition continued to undercut the U.S. balance-of-trade position, exacerbated by the war in Vietnam and heightened social expenditures that fueled U.S. inflation at rates greater than those of trading partners. More than short-run international trade and investment was at stake. Integral to its role as the economic and political leader of the capitalist world, the U.S. government was the head Cold War warrior. As it fought international communism, the U.S. government annually spent millions of dollars abroad on U.S. troops based mostly in Europe and Asia, on military assistance and foreign aid to friendly governments, on clandestine political operations against others, and on open warfare in Korea and Vietnam. Maintaining these large unilateral outflows required a substantial balance of exports over imports, but the surplus in the U.S. balance of trade practically disappeared in the late 1960s and became negative in the early 1970s.

There had been an early post–World War II crisis of an international dollar shortage, and the mechanisms for alleviating the shortage, such as the Marshall Plan and declining U.S. balances of trade, had worked so well that the dollar shortage became its opposite: a crisis of an international dollar glut that eroded general confidence in the dollar's ability to maintain its value vis-à-vis other currencies. Confidence was crucial for its functioning as a key currency, but the U.S. dollar could not devalue, and none of the surplus nations was willing to appreciate its currency to rectify the dollar glut. The Bretton Woods agreements, made at a time when the United States was the principal surplus nation, had deliberately avoided formal provisions to pressure them to do so.

Moreover, some European governments openly accused the U.S. government of exploiting the status of the dollar for its own national interests. President Charles de Gaulle of France claimed that because foreign central banks had to hold increasing balances of unwanted U.S. dollars, the U.S. government was forcing France and other nations to subsidize U.S. transnational corporations' purchase of their economies and to help finance the U.S. war in Vietnam.[2] His cashing in dollars for gold, part of what was called the Gold Rush of '69, was perfectly legal and perfectly uncooperative.

By 1971 the value of U.S. gold reserves was one-third the value of U.S. dollar reserves held in foreign central banks. That was not sustainable. The administration might have induced a mild recession in the United States in order to reduce inflation and make U.S. exports more competitive, but that certainly would have been unpopular a year before presidential and congressional elections. So President Richard Nixon chose domestic political expediency over international obligations, and in August 1971 the U.S. government unilaterally abrogated the Bretton Woods convention by suspending the convertibility of the dollar into gold.

The exchange rate for the U.S. dollar in leading foreign currencies fell almost 20 percent over the next few months, and the price of gold rose. The move, then, effectively punished those nations that had cooperated with the United States by holding unwanted dollars and rewarded the uncooperative nations that cashed in dollars for gold. After a failed effort to reinstate something formal in the place of the dollar exchange standard, leading governments agreed to work with the default position—a flexible exchange rate system for the currencies of the largest traders and investors in the international economy, although one that occasionally involved governmental management. The majority of other currencies remained pegged (that is, fixed) to one of the major currencies—the U.S. dollar, deutschemark, yen, and so on.

Two Consequences of the Demise of Bretton Woods

The devaluation of the dollar gave U.S. producers some measure of protection from imports, but it also had other, unforeseen results.

The Organization of Petroleum Exporting Countries

Since the international price of oil was denominated in U.S. dollars, the devaluation of the dollar reduced the purchasing power of exports by oil-exporting nations. This contributed to galvanizing oil-exporting nations, especially Middle Eastern members of the Organization of Petroleum Exporting Countries (OPEC) that were already unhappy with U.S. support for Israel and the 1973 Yom Kippur War. OPEC declared a temporary oil export boycott in 1973 and then quadrupled the price of oil. It was an extremely successful exercise of market power, and all individuals, corporations, and nations throughout the world with substantial oil deposits, whether or not members of the Organization of Petroleum Exporting Countries, shared in the munificence. The success of the Organization of Petroleum Exporting Countries led to imitation by exporters of copper, bananas, coffee, and other commodities, but none achieved the sought-after cohesion and market power of OPEC.

Thinly populated Middle Eastern nations received large portions of the new bonanza, and these governments used some of the foreign exchange receipts to improve the standards of living of their citizens as well as to spend heavily on luxury goods, including sophisticated weapon systems. Nevertheless, they did not spend all of it and deposited millions and millions of dollars of the enhanced oil receipts ("petrodollars") in large, carefully screened international banks.

Since banks' profits depend on their being able to lend funds at higher interest rates than they pay depositors, these huge new deposits posed a problem. The rise in oil prices that created the deposits also contributed to recessions in the industrialized nations, thus limiting the number of attractive lending opportunities and willing borrowers. In Africa, Asia, and especially Latin America, however, there were many willing borrowers. Import-substituting industrialization policies squeezed primary-product exports to support domestic industrial growth and thereby discouraged export growth, thus limiting both the import capacities necessary for expanding domestic industrial sectors and government revenues. The results in most of these nations were chronic balance-of-trade deficits and large government fiscal deficits, both of which required infusions of hard currencies. In addition to the pressures inherent in import-substituting industrial policies, many of the Third World governments in the 1970s and early 1980s were authoritarian with little popular support, and borrowed money helped sustain a modicum of legitimacy at a time of rising imported oil costs and shrinking exports to the economically depressed industrial nations.

In a sense, then, it all fit together rather neatly. The rise in petroleum prices that weakened Third World nations' export markets and raised their import costs also generated the apparent solution: petrodollars that banks needed to recycle as easy credit. And the commercial banks' initial terms were very easy; peddlers of bank credit pressed everyone in sight, independent of risk or record, to borrow as much as they could be talked into borrowing. And since the borrowers did not have to pretend to adhere to IMF injunctions and bureaucracy, the commercial banks' lending practices temporarily eclipsed IMF authority.

The International Scene in 1979

Vietnam invades Cambodia and topples the murderous Khmer Rouge regime. In response, the People's Republic of China invades northern Vietnam, launching the short and bloody Sino-Vietnamese War.

Shah Mohammad Reza Pahlavi flees Iran, Ayatollah Ruhollah Khomeini returns to Iran, and the Iran hostage crisis begins.

Maurice Bishop leads a successful coup in Grenada, and subsequent instability leads to a 1983 U.S. invasion and change of government.

Tanzanian troops invade Uganda and bring down the Idi Amin regime.

The first black-led government of Rhodesia (Zimbabwe) takes power.

Flight Lieutenant Jerry Rawlings leads a successful military coup in Ghana.

Saddam Hussein becomes president of Iraq.

Nicaraguan dictator General Anastasio Somoza Debayle flees, and the Sandinista revolution is triumphant.

Park Chung-hee, the president of South Korea, is assassinated.

The Soviet Union invades Afghanistan.

OPEC implements its second major petroleum price increase.

The decade of the 1970s was materially difficult for most people in most of the capitalist world. In part due to the termination of the Bretton Woods agreements, which freed national governments to run fiscal deficits unconstrained by fixed exchange rates, and the quadrupling of oil prices and sluggish economic growth, most capitalist economies struggled with high inflation and unemployment, a combination called stagflation. And as the sidebar "The International Scene in 1979" indicates, the year 1979 was a fitting close for an unsatisfactory decade. The administration of President Jimmy Carter never operated as a well-oiled machine, and the demands placed on it by cascading foreign disasters were daunting. President Carter had carried all eleven former

Confederate states in 1976 in his narrow defeat of President Gerald Ford. Well, yes, he is a Georgian, but he was still a Georgian in 1980 when he carried Georgia but not one of the other ten former Confederate states and lost to Ronald Reagan.

The Third World Nations' Debt Crisis

In 1979, the Organization of Petroleum Exporting Countries' second major oil price hike was another blow to Third World nations. Its effects, however, were soon dwarfed by the anti-inflationary policies of the U.S. administration of President Ronald Reagan, elected as part of the conservative electoral tide that swept over industrialized nations in the 1980s. The Reagan administration's anti-inflation policies in the early 1980s, coordinated with the Fed, succeeded in reducing inflation by forcing U.S. short-term interest rates to rise to almost 20 percent. In the process, the policy drove U.S. unemployment rates to the highest levels since the Great Depression and further dampened the demand for Third World exports. A final consequence was that the high-interest-rate policy made U.S. government bonds so attractive that foreign portfolio investment in the United States soared, and the United States became a net debtor for the first time since World War I. The foreign portfolio investment also raised the value of the dollar, discouraged U.S. exports and encouraged imports.

With the sharp rise in interest rates and the increase in the value of the U.S. dollar, Third World debt became more difficult to sustain. Since interest rates on the bank loans to Third World nations were variable (that is, they rose and fell with current interest rates) and since the loans were in U.S. dollars, the rising interest costs along with a more expensive dollar made it harder for debtor governments to meet their loan payments. So although oil prices began to decline in the early 1980s, the combination of weak export markets, record-breaking interest rates, and rising dollar values triggered the debt crisis. Mexico in 1982 was the first to declare openly that it could no longer pay even the interest charges on its foreign debt, and all continental Latin American nations except Colombia and most of the other heavily indebted Third World nations soon followed. The debt crisis had arrived. The resulting credit crunch was eventually transmitted into bursting the speculative bubble within the United States, most dramatically in real estate investments and the failure of over seven hundred savings and loan institutions. The savings and loan failures were due to the popped real estate bubble, bad judgment by loan officers, and a certain amount of outright fraud in the newly deregulated environment. The bailouts cost U.S. taxpayers over $150 billion.

Most of the Third World nations' creditors were large international banks, and the possibility of billions of dollars lent to Third World nations turning into bad debts was said to threaten the survival of the banks and therefore the stability of the entire international financial system. This too-big-to-fail story justified interventions by the metropolitan nations' governments, led by the United States, to save the banks from the consequences of their bad judgment. These governments designated the IMF as the chief collection agent for the big banks, and the alliance among big banks, big governments, and big international financial organizations constituted a formidable combination.

The principal and best-coordinated locus of official international financial power was Washington, D.C., headquarters for the IMF, the World Bank, the Inter-American Development Bank, and the U.S. government. These institutions, aptly dubbed the "Washington Consensus," had a clear idea of the reforms that they wished to promote in Third World nations by using the leverage of the debt. In their agreements with the debtor nations, the Washington Consensus offered longer debt repayment schedules, some new loans, minor discounting of previous debt, and fixed (nonvariable) interest rates in exchange for the governments' commitment to a series of reforms. I have summarized these prescriptions into the following four points with annotations to include some of the Washington Consensus' reasoning.

Fiscal Discipline: There should be no government deficits over one percent of gross domestic product. Since taxes are disincentives for entrepreneurs, tax rates for upper bracket incomes should be no more than "moderate" and government deficit reductions should be achieved principally by restricting expenditures rather by than increasing revenues. Military expenditures, however, are "the ultimate prerogative of sovereign governments" and accordingly not targeted for reductions.

Deregulation: Government controls and subsidies should not distort the free play of market forces. This tenet explicitly included relaxing controls on interest rates, exchange rates, and foreign trade and investment. Deregulation also meant doing away with price controls, subsidized food and public services (e.g., urban transportation and utilities), and workers' protections.

Privatization: Since the production of goods and services is more efficient in private hands, governments should sell existing productive enterprises to private owners and refrain from establishing new ones.

Property Rights: They need to be secured and extended.

The Washington Consensus' reform package became known commonly as Structural Adjustment Programs, and it was very much in line with the IMF's brand of free-market ideology often called "neoliberalism." The prescriptions were also firmly in the IMF's tradition of applying a universal, one-size-fits-all formula for economic problems. The declared purpose of these measures was to produce strongly export-oriented economies that are internationally competitive. The IMF and World Bank touted this goal as the best way to foster long-run economic growth in Third World nations. That is, they contended that the free-market mechanism is the most effective means to promote exports and that a strong export orientation is the most effective source of general economic growth.

Slippery Terms

The terms are rather bewildering. *Liberalism* in the late eighteenth century and nineteenth century celebrated individualism and a free market unencumbered by government rules and regulations. Adam Smith, author of *An Inquiry into the Nature and Causes of the Wealth of Nations* (1776), was a key thinker in this tradition. By the 1930s, however, liberalism became associated with President Roosevelt's New Deal, and into the 1970s and 1980s liberals were those who favored government policies that regulated markets and mitigated unfortunate outcomes. Now *neoliberalism* is a label that is closer to the traditional meaning of individualism and free markets, although neoliberals are occasionally called *neoconservatives*. In regard to the Third World, Washington Consensus policymakers called for "reforms" that meant undoing the regulations and protections called reforms in previous decades. *Structural*, as in Structural Adjustment, refers to freeing markets from controls, although until the 1980s the term was identified with opposition to free-market policies. What can I say?

While the actual relationships among unregulated markets, export promotion of primary products, and economic growth are murky at best, it is crystal clear that the policy prescriptions coincide precisely, perhaps uniquely, with what was necessary for Third World debt repayment to the large international banks. Downsizing government releases resources for debt payment, and Third World governments could pay off the loans to the banks in hard currencies if and only if they were able to run significant surpluses of exports over imports for extended periods. The 1980s were dubbed "the lost decade" in Latin America, with stagnant GDPs and declining per capita incomes through most of the decade.

By the beginning of the 1990s, the debts had not gone away, but the debt crisis had been tamed into a debt burden that was seen to be a problem only for individual Third World nations.

Sporadic debt relief offered some genuine (albeit limited) respite for some of the world's poorest, but three continuing legacies of the debt crisis and Structural Adjustment Programs were clear: The Third World nations had been more tightly integrated into the globalized economy; employers were in a much stronger position than workers; and Third World governments' ability to act positively to shape their nations' economic futures had been weakened. The point here is that these outcomes were carefully engineered and not some "natural" result of globalizing market relations.

The Beginnings of the Socialist World's Entry into the Global Capitalist Economy

From the 1920s to the 1970s, the centrally planned ("command economy") of the Soviet Union ruthlessly transformed a rural, backward, and war-torn society into an industrial nation with substantial education, health, and social welfare provisions and world-class cultural, scientific, and military establishments. And it did this in five decades, which included the ravages of two world wars.

Economic Stagnation in the Soviet Union

By the 1970s it was clear to many in the Soviet leadership that the institutional arrangements of a highly centralized command economy and authoritarian politics suitable for rapid industrialization were ill suited for taking the next step: operating the economy along the lines of mass production and mass consumption. It is crucial to reiterate, however, that the exhaustion of the Soviet model was due to the command economy's unprecedented *success* in having created an industrial base, transportation and communication networks, monetized market economies, and workforces that to a substantial degree were literate, urban, healthy, and disciplined to modern work.

After the 1953 death of Joseph Stalin, there had been some relaxation of the obsessive drive for industrial growth and centralized controls. Planners allowed the production of more consumer goods and the construction of more housing, plant managers were given increased latitude in decision making, and industrial and agricultural workers' wages rose. In addition, the Soviets opened up foreign trade with both communist and noncommunist nations. Trade was three times more important for the Soviet economy in 1973 than it was in 1950, although, at 3.8 percent in 1973, it was still very low by world standards.

There were, however, severe political limits on reforms. Plant managers and workers resisted moving toward a more competitive environment. Both groups did not want to face the riskier environment that threatened unemployment and uncertainty in health care and pensions. Like industrial managers, agricultural managers and farmers pushed back against the uncertainties of more market-driven arrangements. These managers made up a politically potent segment of the Communist Party. The military establishment was very uneasy about loosening strict restraints in economics and politics, and of course members of the bureaucracy had a strong interest in preserving the status quo. These forces opposed domestic reforms and reacted sharply to Czechoslovakian reforms by invading Czechoslovakia in 1968 to crush them. On the other hand, Hungary had gone further down the reform road than Czechoslovakia, but reactionary Soviets did not appear threatened by them.

Travails in China

Between 1955 and the early 1970s, China vacillated between an extreme form of Stalinist centralization and a moderate use of markets and private initiative. The first Five-Year Plan (1952–1957) reversed initial land reforms and distributions by organizing the rural population (around 80 percent of the population) into medium-sized collective farms. The transition went more smoothly than in the Soviet Union, but it still disrupted the lives of several million people. This Five-Year Plan strained relations with post-Stalin Soviets and Nikita Khrushchev's de-Stalinization efforts and early attempts at decentralizing reforms. These political issues, combined with disputes over Sino-Soviet borders and loan repayment scheduling, led to a serious rupture in Sino-Soviet relations, and the Soviets cut off future loans and recalled their technicians who had been aiding the construction and operation of Chinese factories and infrastructure.

The second Five-Year Plan (1958–1963) was even rockier. It included the Great Leap Forward to reinvigorate revolutionary fervor by combining the rural cooperatives into huge communes, some including as many as tens of thousands of people. Another aspiration was to establish small-scale iron and steel production in the countryside as an alternative to the Soviet strategy of emphasizing large-scale plants in intermediate products such as steel, rubber, glass, chemicals, and plastics. These ungainly communes, combined with the use of unproven new agricultural techniques, reduced agricultural production to the point that by 1960 between fifteen and thirty million people are estimated to have died from starvation.

The disastrous famine and resistance by peasants forced the leadership to break up the communes and allow the development of more decentralized configurations that depended on private incentives. Agricultural production recovered, but Mao Zedong (occasionally spelled Mao Tse-tung) and his allies abhorred increasing corruption, growing individual and regional inequalities, and perhaps most, the efforts of critics of the Great Leap Forward to marginalize Mao politically. In response to these problems, Mao declared the Cultural Revolution in 1966, ostensibly as a purifying moment for the revolution. The resulting three years of drastic leveling, forced relocations, and chaotic vigilantism and violence almost tore China apart, paralyzing it politically and economically. By the early 1970s, agriculture returned to the organization and decentralization of the early 1960s, and Mao's political influence, along with his health, waned. He died in 1976.

The new vitality of the agricultural sector, increased prosperity in the countryside, and relatively consistent and permissive policies toward business entrepreneurship galvanized economic activity throughout the general economy, and by the 1980s the output of China's private manufacturing sector threatened to overtake the state-owned and -operated factories.

The new permissiveness in private economic activities did not, however, carry over to the political realm, where a firm lid was kept on political dissidence or any sort of public non-party activity, including religious practices, that might affect the monopoly of political power held by the Communist Party. The political liberalization proceeding in Russia, the former Soviet republics, Eastern Europe, and Southeast Europe was especially threatening to the Chinese leadership, and its reaction to the prodemocracy demonstrations held for months in Beijing's Tiananmen Square in the spring of 1989 unambiguously demonstrated the determination of the Communist Party to maintain its monopoly of political power by any means necessary. Chinese army soldiers and tanks killed an unknown number of protestors, perhaps between one and two thousand, and buried them in unmarked mass graves the same night. The Chinese government continued to crack down on dissidence in Beijing and other cities, arresting and executing suspected troublemakers.

The newly rich and super rich posed a different political control problem for the Chinese Communist Party. Although the Chinese leadership had become comfortable with the increasing economic inequality that came with more market-oriented activity, they had a similar approach to the local rich as the post-1991 Russian regimes had toward the so-called oligarchs: zero tolerance of the private-sector wealthy not paying taxes or meddling in politics. Crossing these lines, which have never been all that clear, could be very dangerous in both places.

Socialism's difficulties in dealing with complex, advanced economies with their pressure for mass consumption was clear in Russia, and the politically inspired Great Leap Forward and Cultural Revolution were disasters and suggest the dangers of authoritarian rule, which in the 1970s also characterized most Third World nations in the capitalist camp. On the other hand, socialism in the Soviet Union, China, Vietnam, and Cuba did demonstrate an ability to lessen material disparities among citizens, reduce hunger and malnutrition (the Great Leap Forward notwithstanding), enhance health care (higher life expectancies and lower infant mortalities), and improve access to education. In regard to the classical liberal goals of democracy and individual freedoms, the jury is still out.

4

The New International Economy and the Dissolution of U.S. Modern Times, 1970s to 1990s

Shifts in the nature of industrial production and the introduction of new products contributed to the transformation of the Modern Times political economy in the last three decades of the twentieth century, but they were not the principal forces. The central source of change came from the economic relations among the capitalist economies. These relations affected the U.S. economy in ways as radical and far-reaching as the watershed changes of the 1930s and in turn reflected back into the organization of the international economy.

Internal Strains of U.S. Modern Times

Primarily through public expenditures, U.S. public policy struggled to contain the centrifugal forces embodied in Modern Times development by promoting economic growth in the Core Sector and sustaining political legitimacy or at least quiescence through social programs. But striking a workable balance between economic growth and social stability became increasingly expensive as economic growth increased the divergence between the Core and Competitive Sectors.

Tax revolts began in the late 1970s, and the U.S. federal budget deficit ballooned in the 1980s. After three years of federal budget surpluses (1979–1981), the three presidential terms of Ronald Reagan and George H. W. Bush (1981–1993) increased the national debt from 33 percent of GDP to 66 percent of GDP, doubling the per capita national debt. This hemorrhage of debt was due principally to the Reagan tax cuts that favored the rich and did not pay for themselves and to massive rises in military expenditures. Budget director David Stockman and other senior advisers to the Reagan administration advocated deliberately pumping up government debt through tax cuts and expenditures in order to frighten the citizenry into sharply curtailing the government's ability to craft and implement effective policy—a tactic they called "starving the beast." Conspiracy theories make me uneasy, but there is evidence that such a mind-set did emerge in the 1980s, and we are seeing some of its consequences in 2011.

State and local government components of public debt along with private corporate, mortgage, and consumer debt also grew massively. Toward the end of the 1980s, the tremendous increase in international sources of investment made borrowing easy and rather inexpensive even in the United States, which chronically had the lowest savings ratios of any industrialized country. Moreover, this increase in total debt meant a corresponding increase in debt payments to lenders—banks, other financial institutions, and individual investors—and promoted the development of a financial industry that was far-reaching in scope, voracious in appetite, and increasingly free from regulatory control.

Until 1981, income from interest payments had surpassed corporate profits in only one year since the first year of official national account statistics (1929), and that was in 1933, the depth of the Depression. The shift in sources of property income from profits to interest (that is, from production to financial transactions) suggests a change in the economic center of political gravity. In the 1980s and early 1990s, fears of inflation were registered in monetary policies, and bankers and other creditors, with assets committed to bonds and other debt instruments fixed in dollar terms, strongly favored price stability over growth (and therefore profits) that might have brought inflation with it. Those whose income and position is predicated on equity (profits and capital gains)—traditional capitalist elites—lost ground to financial interests.

The three-sector analysis of the segmented economy—Core, Competitive, and Public—is a valuable way to highlight the sharply different experiences of different groups of workers and to show how some of the key domestic arrangements necessary for the reproduction of U.S. Modern Times became weaknesses as they worked themselves out. For instance, economic growth during the 1950s and 1960s, along with unemployment insurance, reduced the threat of unemployment, encouraged a series of strikes in the Core Sector, and fostered a decline in labor productivity that corporate managers believed required new and intensified efforts to control labor.

There was quite a bit of excitement in the 1970s and early 1980s about new kinds of work organization that would encourage workers to work harder. These ranged from worker self-management plans, corporate stock options for workers, various kinds of teamwork, and quality of work life (QWL) efforts. By the 1990s, however, after workers throughout the world became available to U.S. employers, the balance of bargaining power tipped and discussion of these experiments declined. The believable threat of job loss is enough to keep workers in line.

In the three post–World War II decades, economic expansion, broadly gauged increases in employment, and the fuller development of social programs, many oriented to children and older citizens, enabled record numbers of women to enter the peacetime wage labor force, mostly in the Competitive Sector or in gender-segregated occupations in the Core and Public Sectors. Women's greatest opportunities for professional employment were in the Public Sector, where more effective fair employment and promotion practices were in place. The prosperity and optimism of the period, in conjunction with a Public Sector politically empowered to regulate social processes to maintain social peace, also encouraged those excluded for reasons of race and gender from many occupations, schools, and public services and accommodations to struggle against discrimination. The successes of the civil rights and women's movements, as uneven as they were, bred deep resentments among large segments of white men.

Employment in the Core Sector chronically lagged behind output growth, and employment opportunities in the Public Sector and even in the Competitive Sector were too few for the new entrants to the workforce. The consequence was a growing underclass that appeared in the cities, an underclass whose poverty was due not to an exploitation that enabled greater accumulation and growth but rather to their labor's not being needed for profits. That is, this was not the type of poverty that promoted higher profits, as was workers' poverty in the nineteenth century; rather, it was a poverty that resulted from some people's being outside of and irrelevant to the circuits of profit-driven production.

There is no question that these internal, dialectical pressures were (and in some cases continue to be) vitally important, but the principal forces for economic change within the United States came out of transformations of the international political economy.

Changing Capital-Capital Relationships

The insulation of U.S. Core Sector capital from international competition in the immediate post–World War II years enabled tacit agreements among the oligopolies in Core Sector markets that reduced capital-capital price competition in the Core Sector. The oligopolistic organization of domestic product markets in the Core Sector paved the way for the next step: establishing relatively peaceful and mutually advantageous relationships with industry-wide unions—once those unions' agendas and personnel had been cleared of leftist influences through the Taft-Hartley Act (1947) and subsequent political purges. Because, and only because, U.S. Core producers had no effective international competition, the peculiar capital-capital relationship could emerge and form the foundation for the capital-labor accord in the Core Sector.

The capital-capital and labor-capital accords had political implications, creating the era of the liberal corporation. It was in the interests of large Core corporations to ally with unions to urge the extension of public benefits, services, and protections for U.S. workers and the poor (the Public Sector–citizen accord) as well as to promote Third World economic development along capitalist lines. This strategy dampened some social disruption, disadvantaged small firms, socialized some costs, and expanded markets. The Council on Foreign Relations and the Committee for Economic Development were two of the most influential forums in which leaders of the largest U.S. Core firms debated appropriate policies. These organizations' memberships and policy preferences were distinct from the antigovernment National Association of Manufacturers and the U.S. Chambers of Commerce, which represented smaller, domestically oriented firms whose more competitive markets did not allow passing on to consumers the increased tax costs of social policies.

The political and economic institutions of Germany and Japan were based on more strongly centralized institutions that politically coordinated capital-capital and capital-labor relationships to maintain economic growth and social peace without the nuisance of antitrust laws. These institutions, legacies of the character of their nineteenth- and early twentieth-century industrial development, proved capable of adapting to electoral politics, and their economies rapidly became tough competitors in international markets for modern consumer goods and intermediate products. South Korea's and Taiwan's brand of authoritarian politics supported successful export-promotion programs and also became serious market competitors.

In describing the demise of the Bretton Woods agreement in the last chapter, I emphasized foreign firms' penetration of U.S. and foreign markets. Because my point was about the resulting deterioration of the U.S. balance of trade that forced the debility of the dollar exchange standard, the general, aggregate level of the discussion—balances of trade, balances of payments—was appropriate. But the effects of the foreign competition went far beyond balance-of-payments problems, requiring industry-level analyses.

U.S. firms had been on the defensive in respect to international competition in such products as textiles, apparel, shoes, and toys for some time. But the foreign penetration of U.S. manufacturing markets beginning in the 1960s was facilitated by cost-reducing advances in communications (telecommunications, computers, and satellites) and transportation (containerization, supertankers, and air cargo networks) and by increasingly integrated international financial markets, and it was a qualitatively different process. Foreign firms were increasingly competing, and competing successfully, with U.S. producers in such Core manufacturing lines as automobiles, steel, and electrical appliances. It was becoming clear that U.S. international preeminence in these and other Core Sector product lines—necessary for U.S. Modern Times as we knew it—was over and that new sets of relationships and rhythms were emerging.

Table 4.1A shows how hard and fast new foreign competition struck U.S. Core manufacturing. In addition to the products listed, imports by the mid-1970s had risen to about half of U.S. consumption of sewing machines, motorcycles, and bicycles, and the proportions of imports were high and growing in important branches of chemicals, pharmaceuticals, and especially electronics. Imported steel had supplied less than 5 percent of the U.S. market in the late 1950s, but that proportion rose to 40 percent in 1982, and domestic steel production declined precipitously.

In addition, foreign-made components could be shipped into the United States with fewer restrictions than on final products. In a few years, television receivers and automobiles with high proportions of foreign-made parts were being assembled in the United States. Some of this movement of foreign firms into the United States ("transplants") was in cooperation with U.S. firms (for example, the GM-Toyota and Ford-Mazda joint ventures), but in any case, the competitive threat from without had, to a goodly degree, moved within.

As table 4.1B shows, foreign firms domiciled in the United States accounted for almost 15 percent of U.S. manufactured out-

Table 4.1.   Imports and Transplant Production

A. Imports as a Percentage of U.S. Sales by Product

	1959	1976
Radios and Televisions	1%	43%
Automobiles	6%	20%
Tires and Tubes	1%	12%
Textile Machinery	5%	30%

Source: U.S. Department of Commerce, *U.S. Commodity Exports and Imports as Related to Output, 1960 & 1959* (Washington, DC: U.S. Government Printing Office, 1962), 19–33; and U.S. Department of Commerce, *U.S. Commodity Exports and Imports as Related to Output, 1976 & 1975* (Washington, DC: U.S. Government Printing Office, 1962), 18–20.

B. Percentage of U.S. Manufacturing Production by Foreign-Owned Transplants, 1990

Chemicals	32%
Rubber and Plastics	19%
Stone, Clay, and Glass	25%
Primary Metals	19%
Electronics and Electrical Equipment	16%
Passenger Cars	13%
Industrial Machinery and Equipment	12%
Total U.S. Manufacturing Production	15%

Source: U.S. Department of Commerce, *Survey of Current Business* 74, no. 1 (1994): 53–59.

put by 1990, and this was in addition to imports of competitive finished products. My favorite example of the confusion is that 75 percent of the value of the 2001 Honda Civic and 60 percent of the 2001 Ford Escort were made in the United States. Such transplant production and the extensive use of imported components and foreign assembling by U.S. firms has made "Buy American" an empty slogan.

The price competitiveness of U.S. Core Sector markets increased markedly, and the effects were much more significant than reduced sales, profits, and employment. By transforming the Core Sector's capital-capital relationship that underlay the Modern Times moment, the new price competition irrevocably altered the structure of the U.S. economy and led to the demise of Modern Times as we have understood it and to the reorganization of the international economy.

U.S. Core firms were involuntarily pulled kicking and screaming into the newly competitive market environment during the 1970s and 1980s, and they indulged in successive waves of mergers that was a part of a general orgy of speculative activity, including real estate ventures, Third World debt, and acquisitions financed by junk bonds.

The New International Economy

A number of U.S. firms responded productively to the newly competitive milieu by adopting some shop floor reorganizations, robotic production technologies, and such devices as just-in-time inventory control. Their principal response, however, was to make systematic and aggressive efforts to reduce labor costs. These efforts included employers' forcing givebacks and other concessions from employees, but firms went beyond reducing current workers' wages and sought labor with lower wages and benefits and without expensive health, safety, and other labor protections. This is the time that companies began to increase contracted outwork and to move operations within the United States from highly unionized areas of the rustbelt (the Great Lakes to New England) to the sunbelt (the U.S. South and Southwest) with little union strength. The major tactic, however, was to relocate production abroad, where in addition to lower direct and indirect labor costs, there were numerous other cost-saving advantages, such as the ability to operate without regard to environmental damage.

The first important wave of the late 1960s did not go very far; the highly publicized *maquiladoras* were just over the U.S. border in Mexico. In a few years, however, U.S. firms initiated large-scale movements of assembly production to the Caribbean, northern Latin America, and especially Southeast Asia in search of low wages and what were perceived to be docile workers, facilitated by continuing declines in transportation and communication costs.

The initial pattern was for a firm to export U.S.-made components to a foreign subsidiary for assembly and packaging—the most labor-intensive stages of the production process—and then import the assembled and packaged product back into the United States. Under special provisions of the customs code, U.S.-made components are not subject to duty, and what is subject to duty—the value added to them by foreign assembling and packaging—are intrafirm transfers easily undervalued for tax purposes. Although Japanese firms using East and Southeast Asian labor for the assembly of exports were pioneers in this pattern, when U.S. firms began to adopt foreign assembly, the weight of the U.S. economy in the world was such that what had been sporadic forays became a new international system of production.

A consistent aspect of this geographic decentralization of manufacturing production has been the use of women workers. And in considering this, one must realize that low-wage labor is not the same as unskilled labor. In explaining employers' preference for women workers, it is important to avoid a "psychology of women" even when it does not deteriorate into essentialism. The key phenomenon is that women have less social and political power and thus are vulnerable to exploitation no matter what skills they have. This is the "secret" behind employers' disproportionate hiring of women workers.

Apparel and electronics products dominated foreign assembly production in the 1970s, but continuing innovations in transportation, communication, and production technology increased the feasibility of producing a wider range of industrial products and parts abroad. The technology of Core corporations during Modern Times promoted long runs of only slowly changing products that enabled lower average production costs through economies of large-scale production and made it likely that there were cost advantages from internal (to the firm) production of components as well. By the 1970s and 1980s, however, it was becoming evident that less rigid production processes were reducing economies of scale in production and allowing economies of scope—flexible production processes that can rapidly and inexpensively be reconfigured to produce differently designed goods. These innovations make shorter production runs economically feasible.

Flexible production technologies were in part a response to new market opportunities in which increasing concentrations of income throughout the world were heightening demand for less standardized, more specialized products. As the system became better tuned, flexible production processes and growing markets for niche products with short product life cycles encouraged greater use of foreign-origin components, routinized more of the production process, and promoted a variety of short-term outsourcing arrangements.

While the changes underlying the New International Economy have increased smaller firms' participation in international trade and investment, there has not been a significant reduction in concentrated economic influence. One cannot mistake geographical dispersion and competitive markets for dispersion of control; large corporations are still the major players. Innovations in information and control technologies that lessened the cost advantages of large-scale operations in production were the same ones that have heightened the cost advantages of large-scale operations in financing, communications, and marketing, which includes product design and brand-name identification. The shift in the ways in which firms could reap economies of scale, then, means that while U.S. firms sometimes own foreign production sites, there is a considerable variation in ownership of foreign plants producing items with U.S. brands. There frequently is no more than a contractual (albeit often captive) relationship with a local national or with an entrepreneur from elsewhere (such as a Taiwanese firm in Nicaragua). For instance, Benetton, Schwinn, and Nike are U.S. firms with prominent brand names that do not own any production facilities but design and market goods produced by foreign contractors, and Walmart and Kmart, giant discount retailers, are increasingly contracting directly with foreign producers in a similar manner.

What began as the foreign assembly of a few products for U.S. markets became generalized into a complex web of geographically dispersed production in which U.S. and other industrialized nations' firms systematically integrate Third World labor into manufacturing for all markets. This is the new international system of production, variously labeled the New International Division of Labor, Global Capitalism, Post-Imperialism, Commodity Chains, or the Global Factory by those trying to bring some systematic understanding to the new international economic order. In this new order, the division of labor is defined by stages of production rather than by types of products. Moreover, the division of labor is extremely fluid, since the spatial patterns of stage or component production can shift frequently from region to region.

Although I have emphasized outsourcing to foreign sites, corporations also outsource some of their work domestically. As large manufacturing corporations have reorganized ("restructured" or "downsized") themselves, they have tended to contract out for a range of services that they had previously done in-house with their own employees. For example, let's say that an automobile firm hired people directly to provide such services as security, accounting, cleaning, hauling, and advertising. After encountering strong foreign and domestic competition, however, the firm becomes leaner and meaner by firing all of those folks and contracting out for the five sets of services with independent specialized firms that are likely to pay lower wages to nonunionized workers and not provide health and pension benefits.

The prevalence of outsourcing means that the gee-whiz figures about the decline of employment in U.S. manufacturing exaggerate the actual declines. In 1980, 22 percent of the U.S. workforce was employed in manufacturing, and at the end of the 2000s, the proportion had declined to around 8 percent. In the example above, those people performing the five sets of services were counted as working in the automobile manufacturing sector, but when the services are outsourced to private firms, bean counters in the Bureau of Labor Statistics consider the workers performing those same functions for the same firm as being in different parts of the service sector. This does not, however, account for all that much of the decline in manufacturing employment, which is real and large.

A general indication of the decline of U.S. manufacturing is that in the last few years, a number of familiar products have ceased to be produced in the United States: incandescent light bulbs, cell phones, laptop computers, minivans, stainless steel flatware (spoons and forks), stainless steel rebar, vending machines, and canned sardines. The proportion of imported components of U.S. manufactures has risen from 17 percent in 1997 to 25 percent twelve years later. A final indicator of the decline is that in 1965 industrial production (manufacturing, utilities, and mining) constituted around 26 percent of U.S. GDP, and by 2009 that proportion had declined to a bit over 11 percent.

But before panicking, understand that the value of U.S. manufacturing output, corrected for inflation, has grown relatively steadily in the last four decades, increasing more than two and half times between 1970 and 2007 (before the current self-inflicted recession). Among the eight largest manufacturing producers, only China's industrial growth, miniscule in 1970, outpaced the United States, but the value of China's manufacturing production was still less than half of the U.S. output in 2007. So while the manufacturing workforce and manufacturing's proportion of total production have declined, the absolute value of U.S. manufacturing has grown, and grown at more robust levels than six of the seven other largest manufacturing economies. Labor productivity has risen, enabling downsizing while increasing output (but not wages), but other sectors have grown more rapidly. The category of finance, insurance, and real estate was one of the most vigorous, rising from a little over 14 percent of GDP in 1970 to 21.5 percent in 2009. So the great expansion of a sector that produces nothing tangible and traditionally has supported real production accounts for much of the proportional decline of manufacturing output. The tail not only wags the dog, it has shown the capacity to be dangerous to the dog's health.

One last note about outsourcing is that corporate boards of directors, nominally representing stockholders, routinely outsource guidance and advice about the salaries of the chief executive officer (CEO) and other upper-level corporate executives to specialized salary-setting firms, often picked by the senior officers. No wonder those salaries are so high, a further demonstration of the extent to which corporate management trumps corporate owners. Furthermore, unlike in Modern Times when senior officers typically worked up within a particular corporation, senior officers now float from corporation to corporation and sector to sector. The current CEO of Chrysler Corporation came from The Home Depot, and Boeing's current CEO and chairman of the board came from 3M (formerly Minnesota Mining and Manufacturing Company—Scotch Tape plus a wide range of other products, but no airplanes).

Outsourcing was only one tactic in a general strategy to lower costs. As U.S. Core corporations competed in the domestic and international markets, it was in their interests to "level the playing field," as the expression goes. This meant that U.S. corporations remain convinced that they were encumbered by cost-enhancing rules and regulations governing worker safety, environmental safeguards, tax payments, and other irritants that their foreign competitors did not have.

Deregulation of the U.S. Economy

There are two kinds of deregulation: covert and overt. Covert deregulation occurs when, say, the U.S. president appoints to government agencies people who are incompetent party hacks or people who are strongly opposed to any sort of government regulations restricting the free play of the market. These new leaders often support budget reductions for their agencies. The administrations of President Ronald Reagan did this well, but the administrations of President George W. Bush (2001–2009) developed it into a true art form. Appointments to the Federal Emergency Management Agency, Justice Department, Securities and Exchange Commission, Minerals Management Service, and Food and Drug Administration were only the most blatant examples of covert deregulation.

Overt deregulation requires a public announcement of new rules and/or passing legislation. The initial foray into the most recent rise of overt deregulation began during the administration of President Jimmy Carter and involved airlines and some financial institutions. And President Bill Clinton signed the legislation that repealed the Glass-Steagall Act of 1933, which had seriously hobbled large financial institutions' efforts to engage in wide and diverse types of financial gaming. Deregulation was and continues to be a bipartisan movement.

The track record of deregulation is not without some severe glitches. The deregulation of the savings and loan associations in the 1980s allowed poor judgment and good old-fashioned criminal intent to ruin hundreds of savings and loan associations and to threaten the savings of their depositors. The U.S. Congress and the administration of President George H. W. Bush, in a controversial decision, bailed out the institutions and their depositors at a cost to taxpayers of at least $150 billion.

The airline industry has consolidated but not thrived in the deregulated environment, and railroads have also experienced a set of mergers and acquisitions that has sharply reduced competition in that sector. The direction of change in other deregulated markets, such as media and banking, looks similar. Moreover, the deregulation of the electrical power industry in California, led by the electrical power utilities and then-governor Pete Wilson, proved to be a disaster for customers and disadvantageous for some of the utilities that helped design the deregulation process.

Before the Supreme Court selected George W. Bush to be president in 2000, he indicated in his campaign that he certainly intended to engage in several dimensions of overt deregulation, but the plan was derailed by the terrorist attacks of September 11, 2001, and a host of massive frauds and accounting scandals in large and well regarded corporations. In the first few years of the twenty-first century, journalists, prosecutors, whistle blowers, and others uncovered large-scale frauds and accounting scandals by Enron, Tyco International,

Adelphia, and WorldCom. And the list continued to grow, with new instances of serious misconduct in such major corporations as the Federal Home Loan Mortgage Association (Freddie Mac), HealthSouth, Westar, the Federal National Mortgage Association (Fannie Mae), Nortel Networks, and Refco. In addition, it turned out that major accounting firms' activities contained severe conflicts of interest, stock analysts for brokerage and investment banking firms deliberately lied to their clients, mutual fund traders were caught in unethical trading, and one of the largest insurance companies was rigging bids. This is a wide variety of misdeeds, but they all had one thing in common: they were not the actions of the economically marginal who were bending rules in order to hang on. These were and are transgressions conducted by very prominent and wealthy businesspeople.

The ability of the competitive market to discipline such unbecoming behavior is limited, and it did not take a subtle mind to realize that the first years of the twenty-first century were not a favorable time to weaken business regulation. In fact, the Bush administration allowed the passage of the 2002 Sarbanes-Oxley law that turned a series of unethical practices by auditors and corporate managers into federal crimes.

The point is not that regulation is good and deregulation is bad. The point is that in some circumstances unregulated markets work very well, and in other circumstances they work poorly and can threaten the performance of the entire economy. There is no universal truth in these matters, regardless what economic theory and self-interested advocates purport to demonstrate.

The Newest Transnational Corporation

By investing in or contracting with foreign operations to produce for global markets, the newest transnational corporations (TNCs) differ markedly in a number of ways from the Modern Times TNC, which invested in foreign sites to produce for those foreign markets. The newest TNCs come out of a different set of dynamics within the advanced industrial nations and amid greater competition among firms, and one would expect the rhythms of their expansion and contraction to be distinct from their Modern Times counterparts.

One difference is that investment in offshore assembling involves more small- and middle-sized firms than was typical of Modern Times TNCs, and another is that U.S. firms are significantly less dominant. A third difference is that the new TNCs' foreign direct investment is more oriented toward poor Third World nations than were Modern Times TNCs. Most foreign investment and trade in manufactures, however, still circulate among the industrially advanced nations, and much of the foreign direct investment going into the European Union is to produce for EU markets. But the Third World nations' share has grown disproportionately fast.

Perhaps the most important difference from Modern Times TNCs, however, is that the new manufacturing TNCs have little immediate concern for the economic growth of the region in which the goods are being produced. These firms' chief interest in their foreign locations is as repositories of inexpensive but productive labor along with reasonable transportation facilities and access to U.S. and European markets. In this respect, they are like earlier U.S. foreign direct investment in resource-based exports by Anaconda, Standard Oil, and United Fruit. Substantial local economic growth is likely to be a disadvantage for these export-oriented corporations, because development and change could raise the price of local labor and create political movements and a stronger government apparatus that would not be in the TNCs' interests.

There are still TNCs that produce in and sell to foreign markets such products as soft drinks, cigarettes, and pharmaceuticals or supply such services as fast food, car rentals, finance, entertainment, communication, and transportation. Whether their production is sited in the United States or elsewhere, these firms are still vitally interested in Third World markets' growth, but compared to the 1960s, this is a much diluted set of interests.

Changing Capital-Labor Relationships

One should never discount corporate opportunism in attacking organized labor, but the issue is how corporations and political conservatives have been so successful. The principal reasons are two. First, significant international competition reduced the market power of domestic firms and precluded U.S. corporations from passing on increased labor costs through higher product prices. What had been a convergence of interests between U.S. Core capital and labor—the basis of the capital-labor accord—began to unravel in the late 1960s and early 1970s as international capital-capital competition sharpened.

Second, U.S. workers, including those in the Core Sector, were increasingly thrown into direct competition with worldwide pools of labor from the end of the 1960s. Labor unions were drastically weakened as their market position was undermined by declining government protections, internal union governance problems, and employers' plausible threat of moving jobs, whether to less unionized domestic sites or abroad.

Union membership in the United States plummeted from 33 percent of the nonagricultural labor force in the 1950s to 12.8 percent in 1998 (11.9 percent in 2010). These aggregate figures include Public Sector unionization and thus mask the severity of the decline in private employees' rate of unionization, which had dropped to 9 percent in 1998 (6.9 percent in 2010). It is not a surprise, then, to learn that the number of strikes by units of 1,000 or more workers declined from an average of 269 a year in the 1960s to an average of seventeen a year in the 2000s (five in 2009 and eleven in 2010).

Seeking cheap labor might seem at first to be an anomalous response to international competition, because foreign competitive advantages in Core manufactures (unlike in the Competitive Sector) were due less to lower labor costs than to the application of new production technologies, innovative workplace organizations, robust marketing strategies, and better political coordination. But a new labor-market dynamic was being born in which U.S. production workers' wages stagnated at best while their productivity rose.

When the profitability of off-shore production became evident, U.S. firms' interests in commercial policies to protect domestic markets from imports were further weakened. More and more U.S. producers had growing stakes in allowing products from offshore sites into the United States with little cost or bureaucratic hassle. In some branches of production, Core capital and labor had historically agreed about the desirability of tariffs against foreign competition, but their recent sharp divergence over liberalizing international trade was yet another nail in the coffin of the capital-labor compact. This was starkly illustrated in the early 1990s by the North American Free Trade Agreement (NAFTA), which gave U.S. employers freer access to Mexican labor and ignored U.S. workers' opposition.

It is not a fluke that public employees constitute such a large proportion of current union membership, although their pensions and benefits are under serious attack.[1] In the private sector, strikes by nurses, janitors, teachers, police, airline employees, telephone workers, and United Parcel Service workers have been the most effective. All of these service occupations, public and private, have something in common: they are insulated from international competition by the fact that their work has to be performed on the spot, as it were—they produce "nontradeable goods." Catalogue and e-commerce companies can sell clothes made in Honduras, use telephone operators in Jamaica, and farm out data entry and web design to workers in India. Nevertheless, their packages have to be delivered in the here and now, and that service cannot be imported. In a similar manner, hospitals can bring in Filipina nurses, and janitorial and security service companies can hire immigrants, but the actual services—patient care, cleaning buildings, policing, classroom teaching, transport services, and telephone installation and repair—are not amenable to foreign production. This is a reversal of historical patterns in which industrial workers were at the forefront of worker unionization movements.

Average real hourly wages and weekly earnings for U.S. workers declined between 1970 and 1990, rose slightly between 1995 and 2000, and stagnated more recently. Despite the steady economic growth of most of the 1990s, median income (the halfway point between the highest income receivers and the lowest income receivers of the population) in 1997 was still lower than in 1989. It is not surprising, then, to find that almost half of the reduction in the gender gap in wages was due to declines in men's wages. Legal and illegal immigration into the United States heightened the labor market impact of greater international mobility of capital and products in both Core and Competitive Sectors. The migration has fostered a resurgence of sweatshops in the United States, shops similar to those of the nineteenth-century United States but currently more evocative of Third World relations of production coming to the First World.

"Send Us Your Brightest, Best Trained . . ."

Not all immigrants are low-wage labor, unskilled, or just desperate. There are provisions in the U.S. immigration code (H-1B visas) that allow employers to bring in foreign workers with specialized skills that are needed but supposedly not available in the U.S. labor force. Nursing is an example of an eligible occupation, but employers in the electronics industry have been especially successful in lobbying Congress to allow the immigration of technically proficient workers, who come mostly from Taiwan, China, India, and the former Soviet republics in a semi-indentured status. In addition to concern about a "brain drain" from the countries of origin, many of the immigrant engineers and scientists received free educations in their native lands. This suggests that poor countries' taxpayers are, in effect, subsidizing them, their employers, and the purchasers of computers and other electronic goodies. When laid off due to recession, H-1B workers find themselves in an unpleasant legal limbo.

The other side of the slow or negative growth of wages and salaries was the record-breaking levels of corporate profits in the new settings. The overall concentration of income, led by property income (profits, dividends, capital gains, rent, and interest), increased every year but three between 1968 and the early 1990s. The middle of the income-receiving array, which twenty and thirty years ago included a strong representation of Core production workers, experienced serious erosion. In addition, wealth became more concentrated as well, including tightly concentrated holdings of federal debt.

Rather than buying into the myth that workers' wages reflect their productivity, it is more useful to begin with the idea that average labor productivity represents an approximate upper limit for wages but that actual rates are determined by relative bargaining power between employers and workers. Then employers' ability to shift production to other sites either within the United States or abroad would lead one to expect a decline in unions, a general sagging of U.S. wages, and enhanced earnings by capital.

Downward pressures on earnings were felt not only in blue-collar work. The restructuring and downsizing of corporations in the 1980s and 1990s increased contracting out for clerical services, and U.S. firms often send their data-entry work abroad or outsource it domestically. This general process has reduced and degraded white-collar work, including middle management, and some less rigidity in gendered and racial definitions of job categories and fewer seniority privileges have also contributed to reducing distinctions among jobs. Some lessening of job stereotyping has been due to legislation and more opportunities for women and minorities, and on the other hand, some has been due to fewer opportunities for white men, who have had to seek work in previously sex-stereotyped occupations and to patch together multiple part-time jobs without benefits. "Men's work" has become more like "women's work."

Core Sector capital-labor relationships have become more like those in the Competitive Sector, and as Core Sector firms increasingly take on more features of Competitive Sector firms like McDonald's and Walmart, Core Sector work environments deteriorate. General Motors is a case study of a highly bureaucratic corporation that tried to retain key Modern Times features in a changing economic landscape, and the new landscape would have destroyed the corporation but for a public bailout. Altogether, the assumption that continuing capitalist development in the United States would continue to improve U.S. workers' income and security is in serious doubt.

Public Sector–Citizen Relationships

As international competition sharpened and disciplining labor could be left to what was looking like a permanent buyers' market for labor, the liberal corporation as a political force quietly disappeared and became politically indistinguishable from conservative business groups. The way in which the Modern Times period produced a consumer and taxpayer identity among much of the white male working class meant that their populist anger and anxiety could be deflected toward foreign competitors, African Americans, immigrants, uppity women, and the poor. The ideology of white male victimization, however, has to be, in reality, rather ambivalent about women in the workplace. With lower earnings for men, women's participation in the labor markets becomes ever more financially necessary for families. As a result, many working men are not enthusiastic about confining women to the kitchen and bedroom.

In all this, a special animus is reserved for the government, seen as parasitic and intrusive, and worse, as the protector of the undeserving and the active ally of women and minorities who are given unfair advantages in the job market. The conviction that on balance, government policy is oppressive and necessarily privileges some groups unfairly is deeply embedded in the U.S. individualism derived from classical liberal thought, and such antigovernment sentiments inform the work of writers from all points of the political spectrum. A wide range of Marxists, feminists, neoliberals, postmodernists, hippies, Tea Partiers, militias, and survivalists argue trenchantly against the regulatory authority of the U.S. government, even though they have very different views about whom the Public Sector privileges.[2]

To a large and growing extent, the belief in government regulation and monitoring of markets was replaced by a reliance on competitive market forces to promote society's welfare, security, and freedom. This was a sea change, and it means that those with economic and social advantages could benefit from those advantages by taking advantage of others with little restraint.

In the new era, governments have been able to dilute the force of labor legislation and even to mount explicit attacks on the institution of collective bargaining. At another level, the Reagan administration was, in effect, able to repudiate the Employment Act of 1946 with little political cost when, in the early 1980s, it dragged the United States into the most serious recession since the 1930s in order to fight inflation. And ten years later, it was a Democratic administration, over the fervent opposition of organized labor, that successfully championed NAFTA without meaningful provisions to protect U.S. workers much less the natural environment. As the political parties compete with each other in attacking social insurance, welfare, affirmative action, and other citizens' protections and benefits, the Public Sector–citizen accord of Modern Times, like the related Core Sector accord between capital and labor, is in tatters.

5

The Triumph of Free-Market Global Capitalism, 1990s to 2007

The rise of the new international order was accompanied by a strong resurgence of faith that private competitive markets are the most effective mechanism for improving the material welfare of people in developed metropolitan nations as well as in Africa, Asia, and Latin America. The United States was an ideological leader in this free-market fervor and in its flip side: pervasive skepticism about collective (governmental) efforts to regulate the social order and ameliorate the negative effects of some market outcomes. The free-market mantra was also supported by most of those in the academic discipline of economics, many of whom are following the money. After all, the discipline does stress the central influence of incentives on human behavior.

In the newly competitive international milieu where cost cutting is the rule, the global economic standard is set by those nations with the fewest protections for its citizens and workers. As a result, there is the persistent danger that free international trade will result in a "race to the bottom" as nations compete with each other to lower their producers' costs and remain price competitive in foreign and domestic markets. The potential for (and contribution to) such a race to the bottom is starkly demonstrated by the way that individual states in the United States compete with each other to attract transnational corporations.

They promise docile and nonunionized workers, lax worker and environmental protections, low or zero taxes, few social services, and free land and infrastructure. South Carolina's successful courting of BMW, Mississippi's landing a Toyota plant, and Alabama's strenuous and expensive efforts to obtain a Mercedes plant are good examples.

This chapter discusses some of the implications of free-trade global capitalism. The first section explores how freer international trade changed some important features of the U.S. economy, and the second section describes three deliberate policy choices and one outcome that illustrate the enthusiasm for the free market. The final section raises a question about the role common markets (trading blocs) play in the era of freer trade and concludes by describing the entry of new players in the fluid international economy, players that changed the shape of international commerce and finance and further diluted U.S. influence.

New Dynamics in U.S. Markets

There are several reasons to suspect that accelerated international economic integration over the last two decades along with a sharp decline in market regulation have generated economic patterns significantly different from those of earlier post–World War II decades.

The Inflation-Unemployment Tradeoff

In the first few decades after World War II, inflation appeared to be the consequence of too much aggregate demand and that recession and unemployment were the mirror image—caused by too little aggregate demand. The notion of demand-based causation for inflation and recession, consistent with John Maynard Keynes's *The General Theory of Employment, Interest, and Money* (1936) and refined through observations of the 1950s and 1960s, suggested that public policy must guide aggregate economic activity along a narrow path between the dangers of inflation on one side and recession on the other, and that there are definite trade-offs between the two. That is, the cost of full employment was the toleration of some inflation, and the cost of no or slight inflation is tolerating some underutilization of productive capacity, most notably registered as unemployment.

The problem with this straightforward formulation is that the U.S. economy has generated two kinds of anomalies that undermine the idea of an orderly universe in which relationships between inflation and unemployment are regular, stable, and inverse. The first aberration was that the U.S. economy went through a couple of periods of simultaneous inflation and recession called stagflation.

Stagflation had been a regular feature in several of the more industrialized Latin American nations during the first three post–World War II decades. Stagflation, however, was not evident in the United States until the late 1950s, when its appearance lasted only a short time. In the 1960s, the U.S. economy acted in ways that at least in retrospect appeared reasonable in terms of the conventional poles of excess or insufficient demand. Stagflation came back with a vengeance, however, in the 1970s, and it was more sustained. A decade of a more "normal" inflation-versus-recession relationship again followed in the 1980s, when public policy deliberately created a severe recession with high rates of unemployment that succeeded in breaking inflation.

A new anomaly appeared in the 1990s. Instead of the abnormal appearance of inflation and unemployment together in stagflation, we saw the abnormal *absence* of both inflation and unemployment. During most of the 1990s and the early 2000s, the U.S. economy grew well with low rates of unemployment and inflation.

These abnormalities are not completely mysterious. One possible source of the stagflation of the late 1950s was that the strongly oligopolized core manufacturing sectors (the Core Sector) with their highly organized workforces were in a position to use their market power to push prices up to the point that the majority of the population who did not possess the requisite market power to keep up had to reduce their demand for higher-priced modern consumer goods. This led to unemployment and recession within the same years as the higher prices (inflation) that caused them. Ergo, stagflation.

The stagflation of the 1970s was probably due to the supply-side shock of OPEC's oil embargo and subsequent quadrupling of the price of petroleum. Again, this was a bald use of market power on the supply side, this time to increase the price of the chief source of energy as well as an ingredient of fertilizer, paints, and many chemicals and plastics. This price hike led to inflation as producers in a wide range of markets struggled to recover their newly risen costs, and consequent market disruptions led to bankruptcies, unemployment, and recession with higher prices.

By the 1990s, employers' threats to send their production offshore were real and plausible, and U.S. wages stagnated, relieving employers of the cost-push wage demands of the 1950s. The IMF and Chairman Alan Greenspan of the Federal Reserve System repeatedly evoked the frightening specter of wages and salaries rising and causing some inflation if economic growth did not slow down. Nevertheless, the newly competitive milieu successfully avoided the disaster of increasing wages for working families. In addition to the lack of pressure from wage increases, heightened price competition from foreign producers in Core Sector markets formerly controlled by U.S. oligopolies kept down the domestic prices of goods, while prices of several nontradable services (notably medical) rose.

Price competition in product and labor markets underlay the economic expansion in the 1990s that dampened the inflation-unemployment tradeoff, and the increased concentration of income among the top income receivers in the top brackets generated rising income-tax revenues that created federal budget surpluses. The Fed's policy of low interest rates created easy credit, and credit markets were awash in financial capital seeking short-term profits throughout the world. In addition, the George W. Bush administration's federal deficits, supported by the legislatures' Republican majorities, provided a fiscal stimulus that helped sustain general economic expansion, with a short setback when the technology bubble popped in 2001.

Consuming More Than We Produce

Official reports during the last ten to fifteen years have repeatedly announced that the United States had again an unprecedented balance-of-trade deficit. The current recession, like those before it, reduced the U.S. balance-of-trade deficit a bit, but when there is an eventual recovery, the deficit will probably once again break records. These trade deficits are larger than the unsustainable deficits of the early 1970s that led to the demise of the Bretton Woods system.

Consuming more than one produces is good work if you can get it. How can the United States get away with it? In more concrete terms, why have flexible exchange rates not worked to depreciate the value of the U.S. dollar, curtailing our consumption of foreign-produced goods by raising their prices in U.S. dollars? A depreciation of the U.S. dollar also lowers the prices of our exports in foreign currencies, and thus puts the squeeze on our consumption of domestically produced goods by giving U.S. producers more incentive to send products abroad rather than selling them at home. Some devaluation has happened, but its magnitude has not been large enough to reduce the U.S. deficit in substantial amounts.

Why not? Large and continuing balance-of-trade deficits require compensatory financial flows. And the secret to the continuing strength of the U.S. dollar is that foreign purchases of U.S. financial and real assets—foreign portfolio and direct investments—supply those complementary flows, thus contributing to the strength of the dollar and enabling our continued consumption of foreign goods.

When foreigners have a balance-of-trade surplus with the United States, many firms and governments turn around and lend us their surpluses or invest them in the U.S. economy. This inflow of investment keeps the dollar strong in relation to other currencies and subsidizes our consumption. The U.S. dollar and U.S. economy are safe and (usually) profitable havens in which to park money. The U.S. currency is one, if not the principal, national currency generally accepted as an international medium of exchange, so many foreigners wish to maintain balances of U.S. dollars for their liquidity. The U.S. economy continued to prosper through most of the 1990s and much of the 2000s, with record rates of return in the stock market, giving foreigners incentives to get a piece of the action by buying U.S. stocks.

In its starkest form, the situation allows foreign owners who make profits selling in the U.S. market to plow their profits right back into the United States and keep their assets safe from the workers who make the goods that are so attractive to us.

Foreigners' ownership of U.S. marketable treasury debt rose from less than 20 percent of the total outstanding U.S. government debt held outside U.S. government agencies in 1989 to over 56 percent in 2010, and foreigners held around 20 percent of U.S. corporate bonds and 10 percent of U.S. corporate stock. Governmental ("sovereign") and private buyers in China and Japan have a particular taste for U.S. federal government bonds. In March 2011, China owned $1.1 trillion dollars of outstanding U.S. government debt—almost 10 percent of the total U.S. debt held outside government agencies. Japan held around 9 percent, and the United Kingdom's 5 percent was the next largest holder. The percentages fall off quickly for the rest of the nations.

While liquidity, security, and good returns are never irrelevant, they are not the only advantages of dollar balances for foreign investors. East Asia's massive purchases of U.S. debt and real assets have helped to sustain their large balance-of-trade surpluses with the United States by keeping the price of the U.S. dollar higher in their currencies (and thus their currencies cheaper in U.S. dollars) than it would be without their compensating purchases of federal bonds.

Foreigners' purchases of U.S. Treasury bonds are advantageous for the United States beyond enabling U.S. consumption: such purchases do not crowd out domestic borrowers and investors in U.S. credit markets. That is, if the only source of funding the federal debt were sources within the United States, a nation with the lowest saving rates among industrialized nations, federal debt would be competing with private borrowers. This is not the case, or at least it is mitigated, when foreigners use foreign savings and credit markets to buy U.S. government debt.

Foreign investment is a powerful force in its own right that should not be obscured by focusing narrowly on the balance of trade and comparative advantage. On the other hand, one might say that the United States appears to have a strong comparative advantage in producing and exporting public and private debt that is highly desirable to foreigners. But to say this violates the distinction between trade balances and international financial flows, a distinction firmly rooted in international accounting practices. But that violation does not mean the statement is untrue.

Not all foreign investment in the United States is portfolio investment. There are the transplant factories, such as the Toyota plant in Kentucky. Foreign direct investment also buys existing U.S. firms and other real assets. Foreign ownership of U.S. companies, measured by asset values, tripled between 1996 and 2005. Chrysler Motors, Rockefeller Center, Universal Studios, Ben and Jerry's ice cream, Snapple drinks, Firestone/Bridgestone tire company, Smith & Wesson guns, Stonyfield Farm dairy products, Anheuser Busch Co. of Budweiser fame, Stop & Shop grocery stores, Lucent Technologies, Sodexho (the largest U.S. food service company), Securitas (the largest U.S. private security company), and a number of landmark hotels and banks are highly visible examples of U.S. companies that are currently or were recently owned by foreign investors.

Effectiveness of Fiscal and Monetary Policy

Another major change in the U.S. economy is the manner in which the international integration of product and financial markets has reduced the effectiveness of domestic demand-management tools. On the fiscal policy side, as imports became larger proportions of U.S. purchases, more and more of any increase in domestic demand created by government policies goes to the purchase of imports, leaking off to foreign producers instead of stimulating local production and employment, diluting the economic stimulus. The operations of transnational corporations have become so international that most of the value of many U.S.-branded products are made abroad, so buying a new Ford Fusion, for example, helps the Mexican economy more than the U.S. economy.

In regard to monetary policy, barriers against the instantaneous movement of financial capital declined and the volume of footloose capital seeking the highest short-term rates of return rose, and as a consequence the Fed had less control over U.S. financial markets. Global financial markets increasingly gained influence over the volume and the terms (interest rates) of loanable funds available to U.S. borrowers.

For example, the Fed's efforts to raise short-term interest rates between late 2004 and mid-2006 did not lead to the expected rises in long-term rates. That was, in good part, because the Chinese and Japanese governments invested so much money in long-term U.S. government bonds that they were keeping the bonds' prices up and thus their yields (interest rates) low. In integrated financial markets, low yields on U.S. government bonds held all long-term rates down, including those for mortgages.

The Distribution of Income

The combination of international integration and deregulation affected the distribution of income. As we saw in the last chapter, free trade caused U.S. labor's bargaining power to weaken severely relative to employers, and deregulation allowed new ways and means to earn income from property—ownership of land and capital, real and financial. Table 5.1 is instructive in this regard, although the table is not immediately clear. All income-receiving households are arrayed from the poorest to the richest. Then statisticians/computers counted out the first 20 percent (one-fifth) of households, working up from the poorest, and added up the percentage of total income received by that 20 percent. In 2006 and 2008 the percentage of income received by that first 20 percent was 3.4. And so on for the next 20 percent, accounting for each fifth and also the highest 5 percent, included in the top 20 percent. One more point about the construction of the table: income from capital gains is not included, and since capital gains income accrues disproportionately to the rich, the omission means underreporting the income of the very rich.

Now let's look at the substance of table 5.1. The first thing that sticks out is that the top 5 percent and top 20 percent of income recipients are the only segments to have increased their proportions of total income since 1970. (The top 5 percent of income receivers is the top fourth of the top fifth. Confusing?) The highest fifth of income recipients increased their proportion of personal income from 40.9 percent in 1970 to 50.0 percent in 2008, an increase of 9.1 percentage points. In the same time period, the top 5 percent of income recipients increased their share of total income from 15.6 percent to 21.5 percent, or 5.9 percentage points. This means that those in the top 5 percent of recipients received 65 percent of the entire increased proportions of income accruing to the top 20 percent of income recipients between 1970 and 2008. Another way to indicate how tightly concentrated was income *within* the top groups is to see that, of the 2008 income received by the top 20 percent (one-fifth) of income recipients, 43 percent went to the

Table 5.1. Distribution of Personal Income among Households

		Percent Distribution of Personal Income				
Year	Lowest Fifth	Second Fifth	Middle Fifth	Fourth Fifth	Highest Fifth	Top 5 Percent
1970	5.4	12.2	17.6	23.8	40.9	15.6
2006	3.4	8.6	14.5	22.9	50.5	22.3
2008	3.4	8.6	14.7	23.3	50.0	21.5

Source: U.S. Census Bureau, *Statistical Abstract of the United States: 2000* (Washington, DC: U.S. Government Printing Office, 2000), 471; U.S. Census Bureau, *Statistical Abstract of the United States: 2011* (Washington, DC: U.S. Government Printing Office, 2011), table 693.

top 5 percent, while in 1970, the corresponding proportion was 38 percent. In a similar manner, though this is not in the table, the top 1 percent of income recipients accounted for close to half of the income received among the top 5 percent of income recipients.

Corporate salaries and bonuses are the most visible example of high incomes. Nevertheless, most of the income of the very rich comes from property ownership. And these have been the fastest-growing sources of income as the proportions of total income being earned through wages and salaries have declined. The influence of property income, which is more volatile and sensitive to cyclical fluctuations than wages and salaries, caused the proportions of income in the top groupings to decline between 2006 and 2008, when the Great Recession was beginning.

Wealth is much more concentrated than income, and by wealth here, I am not talking about fancy houses, cars, and boats but about the ownership of productive resources from which property income is derived. For example, Edward Wolff's careful studies of wealth holdings found that in 2007, over 40 percent of financial wealth was held by the wealthiest 1 percent, and the top 20 percent (including that 1 percent) held 93 percent of the total financial wealth. The rhetoric of so-called people's capitalism and the vaunted dispersion of stock ownership among many small holders are simply not consistent with the evidence.

The concentration of income does not, of course, mean that everyone else is receiving less in absolute amounts. The absolute numbers and percentages of families and individuals existing below the official poverty line began to decline in the mid-1990s. By the end of the decade, the percentages were lower than in 1980, but they turned up in 2004 and have again risen since the beginning of the Great Recession.

Neoliberalism in Action

Faith in the free market, along with a good dose of self-interest, guided some key policy choices in the 1990s. Consistent with classical liberalism, the emphasis was negative—remove restrictions on market activity—but there was also some positive institutional construction to make sure that the lack of restrictions stuck.

Reconfiguration of the Soviet Union

Fixations on the efficacy of free markets were especially evident in post-1991 Russia. When the Soviet Union became unglued between 1989 and 1991, the Russians were suddenly vulnerable to the ministrations of the IMF and the Clinton administration, which oversaw the dissolution of Soviet institutions. The most charitable view of the pressures exerted on the prostrate Russian regime is that the foreign advisers saw an open-market economy as natural and that all it would take to create a viable market system was the removal of governmental interference. That is, the transformation was seen to be principally a negative process of getting rid of obstacles to private-market activity. The U.S. government and the IMF therefore ignored the social and cultural conditions necessary for the proper functioning of a modern market economy and disregarded the need to create regulatory institutions similar to the U.S. Federal Reserve System and the Securities and Exchange Commission, a strong judicial system, and a fiscal structure capable of collecting taxes and disbursing public expenditures for national priorities.

Instead, the foreign advisers concentrated on privatization—distributing public assets among a new class of private owners. This emphasis was fully agreeable with those in a position to benefit from the fire sale of state-owned assets—often senior Communist Party members—and it was done in a rush through executive fiat that bypassed and weakened fledgling democratic institutions. As a result, the reforms created a small cadre of the superrich (oligarchs), and the distribution of Russian personal income went from looking like Sweden's to being one of the most uneven in the world. The resulting unstable conditions in finance, production, and marketing encouraged corruption, speculation, and criminal activities more strongly than they did productive investment.

So much of what had been achieved at terrible human cost in Soviet industrialization was squandered. Marshall Goldman, an eminent U.S. expert on Russia, reported that people on Moscow streets were saying, "Everything that the Communists told us about communism was a lie, but everything that they told us about capitalism was true." The massive inequalities, insecurity, loss of public services, authoritarian governance, and rapid decline of life expectancy in Russia continue to have frightening implications for the world as a whole.[1]

The World Trade Organization

Another illustration of free-market fervor, this one in institution building, was the creation of the World Trade Organization (WTO), a new international organization to promote the expansion of free trade. The WTO was established in 1995 out of the Uruguay Round of GATT negotiations, and its purpose is to promote the free movement of goods and services among nations, in good part by policing government policies judged to be illegitimate trade restrictions. This function is quite similar to that of the International Trade Organization proposed by the Bretton Woods conference more than sixty years ago but rejected by the U.S. Congress as conceding too much national sovereignty to a supranational organization. In the 1990s and the first decade of the twenty-first century, however, the U.S. government has been the major supporter of the existence and authority of the WTO. Times do change!

Unlike the GATT, the World Trade Organization does include agricultural products and trade. In one celebrated case, Brazil sued the United States over government subsidies to U.S. cotton farmers. The U.S. government lost but cut a deal with Brazil, paying Brazilian cotton farmers enough to make them happy and retaining the subsidies to U.S. cotton farmers.

Over the years, however, the WTO has gained notoriety for ruling against efforts by some national governments to restrict imports of goods made under conditions that violate protective standards for workers, the environment, and human rights. There is no question that some of these import restrictions were little more than special economic interests dressed up in the garb of universal human rights or ecological protections. But this is tricky stuff. There may be a general rhetorical agreement that clothes made by ten-year-old children chained to sewing machines do not have to be given free access to all markets, but the only WTO provision that allows prohibiting imports for reasons of labor conditions has to do with products made by prisoners. The United States has proposed allowing nations to prohibit imports that involve severe human and ecological degradation, but the Third World nations are adamantly against such rules. As a result, the WTO has preferred ruling against restrictions rather than attempting to draw meaningful lines.

On the other hand, the WTO has been *extremely* cautious about confronting U.S.-sponsored embargoes currently in force against Cuba, North Korea, Iran, and until 2003, Libya and Iraq. These policies certainly sound like trade restrictions, although among these nations, only Cuba is a member of the WTO.

Adios to the Development Project

I have already mentioned the fourth example of free-market certainty in the discussion of Structural Adjustment Programs and the newest transnational corporations. The implosion of the Soviet Union and the end of the Cold War meant that the developed capitalist nations' strategic interests in Third World nations have declined. As a consequence, the U.S. government's earlier foreign aid and tentative support for social and political reforms in Third World nations have all but evaporated. And as noted in chapter 4, the newest transnational corporations have little immediate interest in Third World nations other than as repositories of inexpensive but productive labor along with a reasonable infrastructure (transportation, communications, power, and utilities). To a large extent, the productive labor forces and infrastructures are results of the previous state-led development efforts that neoliberals now represent as failures.

A striking example of this altered context is the marginalization of Africa, not needed now in Cold War competition and of little interest to transnational corporations except for natural resources. But Africa is only an extreme case in the general phenomenon. While metropolitan nations occasionally respond generously to natural disasters such as tsunamis, volcanoes, earthquakes, and floods, their long-run concerns about the people of the poorer countries seem limited to warding off threats of disease and of massive emigrations to more prosperous regions.

The Quandary of Trading Blocs and the Entry of New Trading Partners

The quandary is whether trading blocs are a step in the direction of freer international commerce and finance or a step away. The full-blown entry of China, Russia, India, and Brazil into the mix of significant nations in the international economy has altered the economic and political landscape and the relative position of the United States.

Trading Blocs: Contradictory or Consistent?

In all of the worldwide celebration and promotion of free trade, there exists a significant uncertainty: along with the increasingly free flow of goods, services, and capital across borders, trading blocs are developing. These blocs, often called common markets, are groups of nations that arrange among themselves to give one another special commercial privileges denied to those outside the bloc.[2] For instance, they may have completely free trade within the bloc and a common set of restrictions for all outsiders, a practice that conflicts with general free-trade principles.

The European Union is the oldest and best integrated of the major trading blocs. During the 1980s and 1990s, the EU continued the process of opening borders for greater freedom of movement of goods and people and standardized safety and food regulations. In a qualitatively different step, the new European Central Bank in 2002 issued a common currency, the euro (€), which replaced national currencies in seventeen of the twenty-seven nations—note the asterisks on table 5.2. All of the first fifteen members of the European Union joined in the eurozone except Sweden, Great Britain, and Denmark. In the next chapter we will look at the issues around adopting the new currency, which is not an easy, straightforward process.

As table 5.2 shows, the European Union had a very expansive first decade of the twenty-first century. In 2004 and 2007 twelve new members joined, bringing the total membership to twenty-seven. Ten of the twelve are in eastern and southeastern Europe and were formerly dominated by the Soviet Union during the Cold War; only the island-nations of Cyprus and Malta were not previously communist. There is a bit of double counting in this; what used to be Czechoslovakia is now the Czech Republic and Slovakia, and what used to be Yugoslavia is now a number of nations, of which Slovenia is a member of the European Union and Macedonia is a candidate.

The North American Free Trade Agreement (NAFTA)—among Canada, Mexico, and the United States—is definitely vigorous although established only in 1994.[3] One sign of its vitality is that discussions were underway to expand it to

Table 5.2. European Union Membership by Year of Admission

*Belgium	1957	*Austria	1995
*France	1957	*Finland	1995
*Germany	1957	Sweden	1995
*Italy	1957		
*Luxembourg	1957	*Cyprus	2004
*Netherlands	1957	Czech Republic	2004
		*Estonia	2004
Denmark	1973	Hungary	2004
Great Britain	1973	Latvia	2004
*Ireland	1973	Lithuania	2004
		*Malta	2004
*Greece	1981	Poland	2004
		*Slovakia	2004
*Portugal	1986	*Slovenia	2004
*Spain	1986		
		Bulgaria	2007
		Romania	2007

Note: Candidate countries are Croatia, Iceland, Macedonia, Turkey.
*Indicates members of the eurozone
Source: European Union, "The 27 Member Countries of the European Union," http://europa.eu/about-eu/member-countries/index_en.htm (accessed October 5, 2010).

include all the nations in the Western Hemisphere (except Cuba, of course), but it was opposed by some of the major South American nations and quietly died. Island nations in the Caribbean established the Caribbean Free Trade Area in the mid-1960s and had eleven island-nation members and two nonisland members (Guiana and Belize) by 1971. In 1973, the organization changed its name to The Caribbean Community (CARICOM).

The Asia-Pacific Economic Cooperation (APEC) is much less tightly organized than the EU or NAFTA, but it does have the potential of bringing together nineteen national economies. The United States is a mover and shaker in encouraging a free-trade area of Pacific nations. The Mercado Común del Cono Sur (Mercosur)—among Argentina, Brazil, Paraguay, and Uruguay with Chile and Bolivia as associate members—is another notable initiative along these lines. In addition to these, there are two other common markets in Latin America and three in Africa, none as large or as well consolidated as these others.

The implications of such blocs for the movement toward general free trade are uncertain. Some argue that the accelerated freeing of trade within the blocs will hasten the general process of generalizing free trade throughout the world, and others maintain that blocs are political units that have a stake in sustaining and perhaps enhancing trade restrictions against outsiders.

New Trading Partners

At the end of chapter 3, I briefly described the emergence of China and the Four Asian Tigers—South Korea, Taiwan, Hong Kong, and Singapore—as important players in the international economy. After the disaster of the Cultural Revolution and the political eclipse of Mao Zedong, the Chinese government moved aggressively into manufactured exports for prosperous nations' markets. China's exports grew from one billion dollars in 1978 to fifty billion dollars in 1988 and, as shown in table 5.3, to one and a half trillion dollars in 2008.[4]

Table 5.3. Export Performance for Some Leading Economies, 2008

	Export Values in Billions of Current U.S. Dollars (Percentages of World Total)	Exports as Percentages of GDP	Manufactured Exports as Percentages of Merchandise Exports*	Exports minus Imports as a Percent of GDP	Per Capita Income in Current U.S. Dollars
Brazil	197.9 (1.2%)	14	47	0	7,490
Mexico	291.8 (1.8%)	28	72	−2	10,000
United States	1,300.5 (8.1%)	12*	77	−6	48,190
France	608.7 (3.8%)	26	79	−2	42,190
Germany	1,465.2 (9.1%)	47	83	7	42,800
Great Britain	458.0 (2.8%)	29	74	−4	46,150
Russia	471.8 (2.9%)	31	17	11	9,650
China	1,498.5 (9.3%)	35	93	7	3,060
Hong Kong (China)	370.2 (2.3%)	212	68	11	31,420
India	179.1 (1.1%)	24	64	−6	1,080
Indonesia	139.3 (0.7%)	30	42	1	2,010
Japan	782.3 (4.9%)	18*	90	1	37,930
Malaysia	199.5 (1.2%)	111*	71	20	7,250
Singapore	338.2 (2.1%)	221	76	1	37,650
South Korea	422.0 (2.6%)	53	89	−1	21,570
Taiwan	254.9 (1.5%)	34	NA	4**	32,700
Thailand	177.8 (1.1%)	77	76	8	3,670
Vietnam	62.9 (0.4%)	69	51	−13	890
World Total// Average	16,129.6 (100.0)	29*	72	−6	8,721

Note: If a nation exports a television set assembled locally but completely of imported components, the entire value of the television set, rather than the value added in the nation, is recorded as the nation's export. This is how some nations' exports appear to be more than 100 percent of their GDP.

* Data for 2007

** Current account balance (rather than exports minus imports) as percentage of GDP.

Source: World Bank, *World Development Report, 2010: Development and Climate Change* (Washington, DC: World Bank, 2010), 378–79, 384–87; data for Taiwan: Central Intelligence Agency, *The World Factbook*, https://www.cia.gov/library/publications/the-world-factbook/geos/tw.html (accessed December 27, 2010).

The Four Tigers' governments selectively backed off import-substituting industrialization and generally followed the Japanese model by beginning with inexpensive, labor-intensive manufactured products and graduating to higher quality and more complex products with higher markups. This was not a sudden, radical change. South Korea was careful to continue protecting the production of heavy industrial and chemical products and financial institutions from foreign competition into the 1980s and 1990s, and all four managed to create a manufacturing export platform by not opening domestic markets to imports until they had new employment opportunities for displaced workers. As a result, poverty declined, and the free-market tendencies of generating more sharply skewed distributions of income were moderated. These successes encouraged emulation by others.

Opportunity, however, was more important than successful examples. The four Asian nations' impressive success with sophisticated export manufactures increasingly depended on more experienced, better educated, and higher paid workforces, thus opening space for very low-wage competition in apparel, textiles, furniture, and other products by new entries into the market. By the mid-1990s, China, Malaysia, Thailand, and Indonesia had become firmly integrated into international product and financial markets, frequently with foreign direct investments from Japan and the Four Tigers.

Vietnam is in the back of the pack because the United States only ended its trade embargo in 1994 and Vietnam joined the WTO in 2000. Nevertheless, while it is a very low-income nation, it is growing rapidly using the familiar Asian route, with some differences in details. Vietnam sent 21 percent of its exports to the United States, and this makes it like China but different from the other newer East and Southeast Asia exporters. Those countries sent less than 12 percent of their exports to the United States, and most of their exports went to Asian trading partners. China's share of Vietnam's exports is rising quickly.

Even further back in the pack, the Philippine government tried to shift to an export-oriented policy after ejecting Ferdinand

Marcos, the thirty-year dictator, in 1986. But continuing internal political divisions produced economic stagnation, which has in turn exacerbated political conflicts. The per capita incomes of Thailand and the Philippines were roughly comparable in 1980, but by 2008 Thailand's per capita income was twice that of the Philippines.

Egypt had a similar experience of being unable to galvanize the economy. In the early 1990s, in what was trumpeted as a major reform effort, there was considerable privatization of government-owned firms, although nobody wanted to meddle with the military's firms. The actual reform was merely to sell government-owned firms, many of which were monopolies, to friends, family, and other supporters, creating a very tightly held form of crony capitalism. This contributed to the civil revolt and overthrow of President Hosni Mubarak in March 2011, and it's too early to tell what direction the Egyptian polity and economy are going to go.

China's ability to more than quadruple its GDP in twenty-five years of export orientation was one of the reasons that India embarked on a similar path in the 1990s. In 1970 China's per capita income was roughly equal to that of India, by 2000 it was twice India's, and by 2008 it was three times India's per capita income. The Indian government, threatened and encouraged by China's performance, began a cautious reform program in the mid-1980s, loosening strict licensing requirements on domestic firms and beginning to open the Indian economy to international trade and foreign direct investment. The development of a truly two-party political system in the 1990s contributed to expanding the reforms. It was a surprise that the competitor to Jawaharlal Nehru's Congress Party, the Bharatiya Janata Party, or BJP (a Hindu nationalist party), was willing to continue Congress Party policies in opening India to foreign commerce and finance.

India has a population of over a billion people, and 76 percent of them live on less than two dollars a day. Even with such a vast reserve army of desperate people, a number of Indian analysts are pessimistic about India's ability to utilize them as effectively as China to create a low-wage export platform in low-end consumer goods that could stimulate the rest of the economy. They believe that this lowest rung of an export platform will be impossible to achieve until labor markets in the formal economic sectors are radically deregulated, allowing employers to squeeze their workers much harder.

More optimistic observers argue that India may be able to skip the first steps of conventional export strategies and go immediately to high-technology products that could enable India to attain dynamism from international markets sufficient to energize the entire economy. There definitely are some signs this could happen: exporting low-end software; sending teams abroad to install, customize, and troubleshoot computer hardware and software; receiving subcontracted back-office work (accounting and other record keeping) for foreign corporations; and establishing technologically sophisticated call centers. India's ability to compete along these lines is due to the frequency of English-language fluency and the government's early focus on creating excellent higher-education institutions at the cost of public primary and secondary education. Skeptics have two serious questions about this strategy. Can the current growth in high-technology exports be accelerated? And if so, will these kinds of exports create the large spill-over effects necessary to spur growth in the rest of the economy?

It is probably a mistake to classify India's economic growth in terms of the East and Southeast Asian export-oriented growth model. While reforms have indeed brought India further into the international economy, table 5.3 shows that India's exports in 2008 were barely more than 1 percent of world exports. This need not indicate failure; India continues to contain strongly nationalist proclivities favoring continued emphases on high domestic savings and investment fueled by its huge domestic market. But as in China, the huge domestic market is potentially available, not presently available. The deep poverty of the majority of Indians, especially but not exclusively in rural areas, needs to be ameliorated, and that entails political and social perils far greater than fashioning export-oriented platforms.

Beginning with the 1980s reforms on foreign trade and finance, Russia certainly has established a substantial presence in the international economy. Table 5.3 shows that manufactured goods made up only 17 percent of merchandise exports, and Russia depends to a large degree on the export of nonrenewable resources. Although Russia has used its vast pools of oil and natural gas to good political effect in Europe, it is unclear whether the Russian export sector will serve as a catalyst for the broader domestic economy.

Brazil resembles Russia in its relatively low proportion of manufactured exports, but Brazil's nonmanufactured exports are much more strongly from agriculture: soybeans, sugar, coffee, orange juice, and cellulose. Furthermore, the manufacturing sector is growing rapidly and serves domestic and foreign markets in transport equipment (including automobiles and civilian and military aircraft) and armaments. Brazil has been a leading arms merchant for decades, and the recent rise of spending for the Brazilian military has further spurred the sector's growth. Some of the rationale for the change in domestic priorities was to protect from foreign encroachment the immense undersea reserves of oil and gas recently discovered at the outer edge of Brazil's internationally recognized waters.

Less Than Success

Sub-Saharan Africa, with the partial exception of South Africa, was bypassed by the export-platform industrial growth experienced in Asia. In part, the lack of success in stimulating manufacturing growth was due to national governments applying a severe version of import-substituting industrial policies in settings with vast majorities in rural areas working the land and very weak infrastructures. Strongly squeezing agriculture in order to promote manufacturing in this setting contributes to deepening poverty among the majority with little prospect for general economic dynamism.

The former Soviet Republics that have become nations have also fared poorly, especially those in a line from the Ukraine south and east through Central Asia. Few of the former Soviet Republics have managed even to approach their Soviet-era living standards. The Eastern and Central European nations that retained their national identities despite Soviet domination have done better. With the exception of Romania, their political transitions were remarkably free of violence, and most of them had institutional structures in place that could be adapted to the new order. European Union members invested heavily in them, taking advantage of well-educated and low-wage workforces, and advised their governments on implementing necessary changes and, unlike the former republics, to implement them in a more gradual and orderly manner.

The last category of unsuccessful nations is the so-called failed states. Every year for the last fifty years, the Fund for Peace and the journal *Foreign Policy* have used twelve criteria, such as economic decline, state of public services, security apparatus, human rights, factionalized elites, and so on, to compile an annual Failed States Index. The 2010 index includes seventy nations, ranging from Somalia as the most failed to a tie between Ecuador and Mozambique as the least failed of the failed states. It's a mixed bag, ranging from governments that are rather effective at doing bad things to governments that for all intents and purposes are missing. Any such statistical construction is controversial, and the comments on the *Foreign Policy* webpage reflect technical concerns, political indignation about rankings, and skepticism about the entire endeavor.[5]

This particular index aside, there are failed states, and there is a strong overlap between them and the nations already noted in this subsection. Poor economic performance reinforces political dissatisfaction, dissidence, and violence that in turn reinforce poor economic performance in a continuing downward spiral.

This description of the international economy and the occasional argument about causation and potentials in chapters 4 and 5 have, I hope, suggested the basic shape of modern international commerce and finance as well as some sense of the origins and properties of that shape.

The principal question remaining is, how stable is the entire system?

6

The Twenty-First-Century Quest for a Stable International Economy

The short answer to the question posed at the end of the last chapter is that the new international system, especially the financial side, is not all that stable. Currency speculation is a major destabilizing factor.

Currency Speculation

Currency speculation is as old as different national currencies; as soon as markets for national currencies developed around trading regions, and multiple exchange rates for a range of currencies became common, there were always folks who believed that they could make money on currency speculation that had little to do with the exchange of real goods. And lots of them were right because the risk-gain ratios can be very low.

Making the example realistic but arithmetically simple, let's say that the exchange rate between the Japanese yen (¥) and U.S. dollar ($) is ¥80 for $1, or conversely $0.0125 for ¥1. Some speculators circling around various exchange rates become convinced that the U.S. dollar is likely to decline in value relative to the Japanese yen. They then borrow as many U.S. dollars as they can and convert them to Japanese yen. If the U.S. dollar does decline in price, say to ¥60 to $1, or $0.015 to ¥1, the speculators go back into enough newly cheapened U.S. dollars to pay off their dollar debt and reap a 20 percent profit.

There are two especially sweet aspects to this operation. Once a speculative attack begins, others will sense an opportunity and pile on, often forcing down the yen price of the U.S. dollar even if there had been no real reason for its weakness. The prophecy of a devalued dollar becomes self-fulfilling. And if the U.S. dollar survives the attack and does not change its price with respect to the Japanese yen, the speculators will simply buy dollars at the original exchange rate of ¥80 for $1 and pay off their dollar debt, losing only the fees and interest payments of the loan.

Currency speculation thrives when there is ready access to cross-border portfolio investment, fixed exchange rates, and ease of converting from one currency to another. These conditions appeared in the European Union in the early 1990s, when most EU members pegged their currencies to the German deutschemark. Speculators began attacking Western European currencies in 1992 and succeeded in forcing devaluations on most. This experience probably accelerated the EU effort to create a common currency.

In 1994, the year that NAFTA began, speculators turned to the Mexican peso. Despite $50 billion of instant loans from the U.S. Treasury and the IMF, Mexico had to float its exchange rate, which fell 50 percent in a month. The devaluation caused a crisis in the Mexican banking system, because the banks had borrowed heavily in U.S. financial markets to make domestic loans. The devaluation raised the peso value of their dollar debts and reduced the dollar value of their peso loans, and no matter which way one looks at it, the power of speculative hot money was clear: large-scale currency speculation could force the devaluation of a currency, creating an economic crisis that spawned disruption and instability in the broader international economy.

In the mid-1990s, Thailand, Malaysia, Indonesia, Taiwan, and South Korea were fiscally conservative and politically ungenerous in regard to workers' rights and social policies. The five economies were booming, led by export platforms that generated domestic investment bubbles in stock markets and real estate. Wall Street wanted in on more favorable terms than were then available to foreign investors and pressured the U.S. Treasury to pressure the IMF to pressure the countries to relax their controls on foreign investment. It was not a hard sell anywhere along the line: the U.S. Secretary of the Treasury at that time was Robert Rubin, who had worked twenty-six years as a Goldman Sachs executive, ending as cochairman of the bank; the United States is the only member of the IMF whose vote is large enough to veto any IMF policy; and the small countries are anxious about the likely consequences of irritating the giant international financial institution.

In 1997 speculators took advantage of the newly opened financial systems and attacked Thailand's currency (the baht), and the contagion soon spread to Indonesia, Malaysia, the Philippines, and South Korea. The IMF prescribed its usual recessionary policies: raise interest rates to curb possible inflation, curtail government spending, and refuse aid to their troubled banking systems. Thailand followed the IMF formula closely, and the baht fell 25 percent in one day and broad swathes of the banking and manufacturing sectors failed. It took years to recover, and the political scars are still evident. Indonesia also followed the IMF's advice with results similar to those in Thailand. Political obtuseness by the IMF and the Indonesian government led them to cancel food and fuel subsidies as part of the fiscal austerity program, and the consequent riots brought down the thirty-year authoritarian regime of President Suharto.

The IMF and creditor nations lent the five nations around $100 billion to withstand the speculative attacks, and the loans succeeded only in staving off devaluations until elites and corporations could take advantage of liberalized financial controls and get out of local currencies at favorable rates before the devaluations. Altogether, these currencies devalued around 40 percent.

Malaysia, on the other hand, immediately imposed a twelve-month minimum for repatriating foreign portfolio investment, lowered interest rates, and lent their banks enough liquidity to withstand the worst of a credit crisis. South Korea, China, and

India had stringent currency controls, ignored IMF advice by putting capital into their banks, and weathered the Asian crisis of 1997–1998 fairly well.

The economic slowdown in Asia reduced the price of oil 40 percent, and Russia suddenly found itself vulnerable to similar attacks. As in the early 1990s when the IMF lent billions of dollars to the transitioning economy, the lack of currency controls enabled much of the IMF defensive loans to leave Russia the same day they were received. Rich Russian oligarchs are very adept at asset stripping. The ruble finally crashed in early 2009, and the turmoil adversely affected Eastern Europe, although only the Czech Republic made the mistake of following IMF advice. Brazil also felt echoes of the Asian crisis in 1998 and 1999, and Taiwan and Singapore were hit by some of its backlash in 2000.

Questions about the IMF

Recovery was slow and uneven, and the vulnerability of the system to such panics has forced some serious rethinking about the dangers of an unregulated international economy, or at least an unregulated international financial system. Some of this rethinking has been directed at the IMF, which has been the subject of controversy since its founding. From the 1950s into the 1970s, most criticism had come from Third World leaders and U.S. liberals who disliked the IMF's consistent priorities of paying foreign creditors rather than supporting the interests of local businesses, workers, and the poor.

In another dimension of criticism, the IMF often seemed to be operating as an arm of U.S. foreign policy. For example, the IMF boycotted the Chile of President Salvador Allende but generously supported the brutal regime of General Augusto Pinochet, who overthrew the democratically elected Allende in 1973. Conversely, the IMF lent Anastasio Somoza $66 million just before he was toppled by the 1979 Sandinista revolution, and the IMF refused to deal with the Sandinista government.

Current criticisms of the IMF are different. Mounting evidence of IMF confusion and inappropriate policy prescriptions in Russia and during the Asian crisis made the IMF a target of serious censure. An intriguing aspect of the anti-IMF sentiment is that the most trenchant condemnations of the IMF have come not from longtime liberal and Third World critics but rather from conservative U.S. politicians and economists. The IMF was designed to secure fixed exchange rates, and it has always had trouble dealing with the effects of international investment. In a world of often flexible exchange rates and daily international movements of billions and billions of investment dollars, the IMF may have become an anachronism. In the 1980s the IMF found a new role for itself as the collection agent for the large international banks during the Third World credit crisis, and in doing so, it overshadowed the World Bank as a development institution. The dissolution of the Soviet Union gave the IMF another new task: working with transitional economies moving toward capitalism. As we have noted, the IMF's record in both of these functions has been less than triumphant.

The U.S. Financial Crisis

The debate over the IMF as well as the need to moderate extreme swings in international exchange rates produced by massive movements of short-term speculative capital are important, but the beginnings in 2008 of the current international economic malaise known as the Great Recession eclipsed both concerns. The Great Recession was not due to a speculative currency crisis like that of Mexico, Indonesia, Thailand, and Russia in the 1990s. The genesis of this disaster is rooted principally in the meltdown of the U.S. banking system. As such, it has more in common with the 1980s Third World debt crisis and the U.S. savings and loan collapse as well as Japan's 1992 banking collapse. What all these setbacks have in common is that they were brought about by serious mistakes made by executives in large banks. While most of the disruption was caused by U.S. financial institutions, they were not alone in leaping into overly risky endeavors with inadequate reserves.

Both overt and covert styles of financial deregulation are certainly part of the story, although the prior question is why would tighter controls have been necessary? In a world of low interest rates, banks, mortgage lending companies, insurance companies, and a myriad of other financial institutions sought higher returns than were available by means of traditional practices. Writing mortgages for higher-risk borrowers looked to be an attractive way to increase returns on lending. A short lexicon of these risky financial instruments follows.

Making mortgages of mixed qualities can be problematic, but that is only the beginning. When financial institutions bought a mortgage, they often combined it with whole and pieces of other mortgages into financial instruments known as Collateralized Debt Obligations (CDOs). The underlying mortgages account for the reference to collateral in the name and make CDOs one of a family of derivatives—securities whose values are *derived* from the value of one or more underlying assets. The process of creating these financial instruments is called securitization and was said to reduce risk through diversification. Issuing firms marketed new CDOs primarily to pension funds, hedge funds, mutual funds, and other financial enterprises, charging high fees for the service.

Since CDOs were not traded openly in transparent markets that would allow investors to gauge their market value, the peddlers of sliced and diced CDOs assured investors of their worth by having them rated by one of the major credit-rating firms. Fitch Ratings, Standard & Poor's, and Moody's Investors Service are the three major firms that rate the creditworthiness of all sorts of debt and investment vehicles, and they operate as high-profit oligopolies. The issuers of the financial instruments to be rated directly pay the credit-rating firm for the service. If the issuer does not like the rating and goes elsewhere, the rating firm loses a customer, which is pure conflict of interest. But the issuers of CDOs were not unhappy with the ratings received by their CDOs, because the credit rating firms did not hesitate to assign top ratings (AAA or Aaa) to these poorly understood CDOs. Actually determining the quality of the mortgages underlying CDOs, even if it could be done, is long and expensive, and the ratings firms clearly did not do due diligence. It is not clear why anyone should pay attention to such ratings. It is instructive that the agencies' ratings were believed by even many issuing banks, which were misled about the riskiness of the CDOs and participated directly in the gamble, keeping more CDOs on their books than they had initially intended.

There is one more financial term that you should know even in this brief account. Credit default swaps (swaps) can be thought of as insurance policies. They are contracts between two parties in which one party that has invested in a CDO or other financial vehicle is guaranteed by the second party to pay the loss in case the CDO or other vehicle defaulted. They were not called insurance, however, because that might have tempted some state governments to regulate them. One fascinating feature of swaps is that you do not have to own the actual asset whose future value you're betting against. It's as though you bought a life insurance policy on someone you don't know but suspected to be in ill health. These financial instruments are not about hedging bets in a way that encourages moderate risk taking and investment in, say, new enterprises; CDOs and swaps were designed to generate fees for issuers and to breach accounting standards in order to avoid regulations and taxes.

Much of the investment in CDOs and swaps was financed by massive volumes of borrowed money. The Republican Congress, allied with some leading Democratic Senators, explicitly excluded the new financial instruments from regulation, and in 2004 the Securities and Exchange Commission (SEC), under pressure by the investment banks, relaxed a 12-to-1 debt-to-equity limit for the five largest investment banks—Goldman Sachs, Morgan Stanley, Lehman Brothers, Bear Stearns, and Merrill Lynch—and the ratios rapidly rose to what was called "highly leveraged." The riskiest way to be highly leveraged is to have your debt in short-term borrowing while your assets, like CDOs, were long-term and of dubious liquidity. Many made pots of money using that business model.

So there are the initial mortgages and CDOs, which are bets on the solidity of the mortgages even though it is difficult to figure out how many and which mortgages are in the CDO. The swaps end up being bets against bets, and there were ways to bet on swaps. But I think you get the idea. Swaps were so popular that their dollar volume rose from one million to six trillion dollars between 1998 and 2008. Building on that popularity, several institutions, notably Goldman Sachs, began to bet against CDOs in 2007 if not before, while still creating and selling them to their clients.

The financial markets did not have a monopoly on all the loose and crazy activities and extravagant voracity that was going on. For example, cheap credit fuelled several high-profile and misguided mergers and acquisitions of firms that actually produced something of worth. I focus on the financial markets because that is where the problems began.

The whole house of cards, or rather the section of the house of cards that I've been describing, was based on the continuing rise of housing prices. Everyone, financial professionals and amateurs, "knew" that housing prices were going to continue to rise, and with few exceptions they all piled on. As home prices did continue to rise, there was a wealth effect on consumers. The value of people's houses over and above their mortgages rose, and the value of the stock components of people's defined-contribution retirement accounts, such as 401(k) accounts, also rose. The increased wealth projected many people into a financial comfort zone, even though wages were either declining or stagnant. Homeowners cashed in on their house equity by raising their mortgages, withdrawing the new-found equity for education, medical care, and consumer goods and services, and they were often blasé about credit card debt. The scale of these new equity withdrawals (and debt increases) was huge: 7 percent of the 2007 GDP in the United States.

The prices of the overbuilt housing sector began to soften in 2007 (a bit earlier in some markets), and by 2008 the declines in house prices frightened investors so badly that the same herd instinct behind their earlier enthusiastic investing caused a stampede for the exits and exacerbated the collapse. Credit markets froze, and the value of CDOs, always murky, dropped precipitously as the underlying mortgages became shakier and foreclosures rose, spreading from subprime mortgages to mortgages that initially were solid. With no markets for CDOs, those holding them could not sell them in order to pay the short-term debts incurred to buy them.

Bear Stearns, a highly respected eighty-five-year-old institution that had pioneered securitization, collapsed in early 2008, and the Fed bribed JPMorgan Chase to take it over and dissolve it. In a controversial decision, Bear Stearns' creditors were paid 100 percent of what was owed them; after all, why lose on risky gambles when friends at the Treasury are in charge of the public purse strings?

September 2008 was an exciting month. Lehman Brothers, like Bear Stearns in that it was leveraged around 30 to 1, collapsed in September 2008. U.S. officials decided to let it go through a regular bankruptcy and liquidation without federal help, and the case will probably be fought in the courts for years. Merrill Lynch went under and was sold to Bank of America. Bank of America shareholders accused executives of concealing the deterioration of Merrill Lynch's assets and that the failing institution intended to pay large bonuses to its failed executives.

The American International Group (AIG), the nation's largest insurance company, had issued over $440 billion worth of swaps, and since the underlying CDOs were tanking, the holders of the swaps demanded payment on their insurance policies. In September 2008 AIG ran out of cash and sources of credit, until Congress passed a bill to bail them out to the tune of $85 billion. This turned out to be the down payment of what eventually became an AIG bailout of more than $170 billion. Much of the money went directly to the investment banks holding the swaps, once again paying creditors 100 percent of what was owed them.

Goldman Sachs received the largest share, and the SEC is investigating how Goldman Sachs could have issued $22 billion in new CDOs in 2006 alone and have so many of them turn out to be deeply flawed. Thus the suspicion that Goldman Sachs was issuing these CDOs only to bet against them with swaps. Two weeks after the $85 billion bailout, AIG threw a $440 million party at a California resort for its top executives, and in early 2009 AIG announced that it was awarding $165 million in bonuses to top executives to reward and retain them for almost bringing down the firm.

Also in that same busy September, Washington Mutual was seized by its regulator when depositors withdrew $16.4 million in ten days. The FDIC took receivership of the bank and sold it and its assets to JPMorgan Chase. Finally, in September 2008 federal agencies took direct control of the Federal National Mortgage Association (Fannie Mae) and the Federal Home Loan Mortgage Corporation (Freddie Mack). The federal government had sponsored the two companies in 1968 to guarantee mortgages in order to help people obtain less expensive loans, but they had been operating as fairly autonomous entities. At the time of the takeover, Fannie Mae and Freddie Mack guaranteed or owned about $6 trillion of home loans, around one-half all U.S. residential mortgages, and they were in perilous financial shape.

One last death notice: Wells Fargo bought Wachovia at the very end of 2008. As in all of these takeovers, many lawyers will make comfortable livings off the litigation for years.

Political Responses to the Crisis in the United States

Accurate predictions do not come easily. Early in the housing bubble, Fed Chairman Alan Greenspan and his successor, Ben Bernanke, denied that the extreme price increases in housing needed attention. In the second stage, President George W. Bush, Ben Bernanke, and Treasury Secretary Henry Paulson (another former head of Goldman Sachs) denied in 2007 that the gathering problems in the mortgage-backed securities market would negatively affect the wider economy.

But problems in the mortgage-backed securities market did happen and grievously affected the wider economy. From the second quarter of 2008 to the second quarter of 2009, U.S. GDP experienced an average of almost 4 percent per quarter of negative growth (that's really how they say it). With total job losses around eight million, unemployment rose to over 10 percent, and between October 2007 and the low point in March 2009, the prices of stocks listed on the New York Stock Exchange declined over 50 percent. International trade in goods and services declined 17 percent, most of it in the second half of 2008 and the first quarter of 2009, making it the largest and fastest contraction in four decades. This is why this period is called the Great Recession, clearly an allusion to, but not quite, the Great Depression of the 1930s.

The first major legislative effort to stem the downward spiral was the Stimulus Act of February 2008. The Act cost around $152 billion, and its principal provisions were to send tax rebate checks to most tax payers and provide some tax incentives to businesses. As some predicted, at least half of the rebates went into individuals' savings or toward paying down previously contracted debt rather than stimulating demand for goods and services.

In an effort to make bank bailout policy more expeditious, consistent, and coordinated, Secretary Paulson convinced Congress to pass the Emergency Economic Stabilization Act (October 3, 2008), setting up the Troubled Asset Relief Program (TARP) with $700 billion to inject into financial institutions at the discretion of the secretary of the treasury. The initial approach was to use the funds to buy toxic ("troubled") assets to remove them from banks' balance sheets and inject liquidity. This strategy was soon changed to supply liquidity to the institutions by acquiring equity in the firms, and so taxpayers became part owners of firms rather than owners of financial assets no one wanted. This was a good move, but the fact remained that resources were channeled to the banks and bankers, the cause of the crisis, instead of toward the unemployed and homeowners in trouble, the victims of the crisis.

The criteria for selecting banks for TARP support remain vague, and more than 16 percent of the total went to General Motors and Chrysler—remember that aspect of the mess? Anyway, in regard to banks, one criterion appears to be to finance stronger banks' takeovers of shakier ones. "Too big to fail" is another criterion that is definitely on the list. This has raised calls for limiting financial institutions' size and scope so that if they make too many bad decisions, their demise would not present a threat to the entire financial system. There are a number of ways in which this could be done, but the problem is that the current trend, encouraged by TARP, is *consolidation* of the financial sector around larger institutions. We have seen a number of the largest institutions succumb and be absorbed by equally large firms. And below the headline level, lots of other banks are failing. These failures include local banks being taken over by regional banks, and so on. It's called consolidation and reduces competition among banks.

These expanding financial institutions are not only too big to fail; they are also too politically connected to fail or to be broken up, and they have no incentive to change the behaviors that created the crisis. To the contrary, their executives now know that the federal government believes that they have to be bailed out when their moneymaking casino ways don't work, and when those activities do work, there's lots of money to be made. Not a bad deal for them, but not a good one for taxpayers.

President Obama's American Recovery and Reinvestment Act (often simply called "the stimulus") of February 2009 weighed in at $786 billion, but unlike the TARP, it did not hand out money to friends, neighbors, and former colleagues. There is a Keynesian boldness about its emphasis on investments in infrastructure, such as transportation, education, energy, and health, which are intrinsically important to the economy and society. The nonpartisan Congressional Budget Office reported in 2010 that the stimulus, despite its inadequate size, had created or saved between one and 2.1 million jobs.

This is rather heartening, but there are still serious difficulties. It is not clear that many lost jobs will ever come back. Credit is still not readily available because even financial institutions that received federal bailout money are sitting on it rather than lending. The federal deficit is frightening, caused primarily by the reduction in tax revenues due to President George W. Bush's tax breaks for the rich and the recession. Banks have been unwilling to come through on mortgage readjustments, and the effect of accelerating foreclosures on the housing market will continue for years. There is nothing in place to guard against another excess-and-bust cycle in the financial markets. Congressional politics are dysfunctional. Many frightened legislators and citizens see efforts to save capitalism to be an effort to destroy capitalism and create socialism—echoes of the conservative hysteria during the New Deal.

Each major period of unregulated market activity in the United States has led to greater unevenness of the distribution of income, serious general economic downturns, and eventually periods of serious economic reform. The freewheeling "Gilded Age" of the 1870s and 1880s yielded to the "Progressive Era" with the Interstate Commerce Commission (1887), the Sherman and Clayton antitrust acts (1890 and 1914, respectively), the Food and Drug Administration (1906), the Sixteenth Amendment (1913) that permitted a graduated federal income tax, and the Federal Reserve System (1914). The "Roaring Twenties" ended with a whimper in the decade-long Great Depression of the 1930s and encouraged the passage of the Glass-Steagall Act (1933) preventing financial institutions from engaging in more than a limited number of financial markets, the Wagner Act (1935) protecting workers' rights to organize, and the whole alphabet soup of agencies and regulations of President Franklin D. Roosevelt's New Deal.

In the last thirty or so years, the pendulum of short memories has been swinging back toward a faith in the beneficent operation of markets unfettered by government regulation. The ethically challenged economics profession has generally been a cheerleader of the shift in opinion. This does not mean that such a position is wrong. It simply means that in some circumstances unregulated markets work well, but they do not work well in all circumstances all the time. A better balance is needed.

But by historical standards, the current political response to the crisis brought on by unregulated markets is rather tepid.

The big banks funded by federal bailouts did not spend all the taxpayers' money by rewarding their top executives for driving their firms into the ground. They used a good portion of it to pay for lobbying through such organizations as the American Bankers Association to fight any effort at reregulation. And President Obama's administration is already on record in favor of weakening the Sarbanes-Oxley Act passed in the wake of the corporate scandals in the early 2000s. Moreover, many of the administration's top economic advisers were enthusiastic participants in the Clinton administration's deregulation initiatives, and the administration has proved to be unwilling or unable to counter big-money influence.

The result was the Dodd-Frank Wall Street Reform and Consumer Protection Act, which underwent months of compromises and passed in July 2010. The act restricted banks' use of their own money for speculative investments ("proprietary trading"), established federal oversight of derivatives trading, made ratings agencies accountable for mistakes, and protected financial market consumers. Since implementation is only beginning, and the Securities and Exchange Commission has decided not to enforce the provisions about the ratings agencies, it is difficult to know how seriously the act will be taken. The act is under fire from the bank-sponsored Republican majority in the House of Representatives, so maybe it is more significant than I believe.

The Global Reach of the Great Recession

Not only were U.S. officials' reassurances wrong about the real estate bubble's effect on the U.S. economy, they completely failed to grasp the width, depth, and speed of the consequences for the international economy. The bursting of the mortgage-backed securities bubble was transmitted to foreign economies through three major avenues: toxic U.S. securities held by foreigners; the decline of U.S. demand for imports—goods and services produced abroad; and in the case of nations with large numbers of their workforces abroad, such as Mexico, El Salvador, and Bangladesh, the decline in remittances to families from the emigrating workers. Table 6.1 conveys the patterns of recession in much of the world, comparing recent declines with the Great Depression to show that in many countries the recent contraction of production and income was greater than in the 1930s. Those hit the hardest were the more closely tied to U.S. financial, product, and labor markets, but that is not the entire story. Blaming the United States is a favorite international game, rivaled only by soccer, but some of the most serious setbacks were felt in countries that managed to produce their own crises with little help from the United States.

Europe and the Race to the Bottom

Many traditionally conservative European banks and financial institutions bought into the U.S. casino culture through purchases of CDOs and swaps, and Europeans held almost a quarter of the risky financial instruments issued by U.S. financial institutions. When their values collapsed in 2008 and 2009, European credit markets were crippled but not frozen as in the United States. The European Central Bank effected bailouts similar to those in the United States for the banks in the seventeen-nation eurozone. The central banks of the ten non-eurozone members of the EU, notably Great Britain, also bailed out their banks when needed but imposed stricter conditions on them than in the United States. As a nonmember of the eurozone, the weak British pound mitigated some of the effects on the British economy. Great Britain carries a massive national debt due to large-scale domestic investments in education, health care, and highways in the late 1990s and early 2000s until the recession curtailed tax receipts and a new Conservative government came to power.

Foreign countries as disparate as Iceland, Ireland, Britain, Spain, Eastern Europe, and India also experienced the rapid deflation of housing bubbles, and Iceland, with a population of just

Table 6.1. Largest Peak-to-Trough GDP Change, 2007–2010 and 1928–1935 (Percentage Change in GDP of Larger Economies)

	From 2007 to 2010	From 1928 to 1935		From 2007 to 2010	From 1928 to 1935
Ireland	−14.3	NA	Taiwan	−10.1	−6.2
Turkey	−12.8	NA	Singapore	−9.0	NA
Finland	−9.8	−4.0	Japan	−8.7	−7.3
Sweden	−7.5	−6.2	Hong Kong	−8.0	NA
Denmark	−7.3	−3.6	Thailand	−7.4	NA
Italy	−6.8	−5.5	Malaysia	−6.4	NA
Germany	−6.6	−24.5	South Korea	−4.6	−1.5
Britain	−6.4	−5.8	South Africa	−2.8	NA
Greece	−5.7	−6.5	Kenya	−2.7	NA
Netherlands	−5.2	−7.8	New Zealand	−2.6	−14.6
Austria	−5.0	−22.5	Mexico	−9.1	−20.8
Spain	−4.9	−6.1	Brazil	−4.7	−4.4
Belgium	−4.2	NA	Chile	−4.2	−30.0
France	−3.9	−14.7	United States	−4.1	−28.5
Portugal	−3.8	NA	Canada	−3.4	−29.6
Switzerland	−3.3	−8.0	Peru	−2.1	−25.8
Norway	−2.8	−7.8			

Source: Floyd Norris, "In Great Recession, Other Nations Have Suffered More," *New York Times* (September 18, 2010), B3; Angus Maddison, *Monitoring the World Economy, 1820–1992* (Paris: Development Centre, OECD, 1995), 69.

over 300,000, was one of the first countries to run into serious financial trouble. The Icelandic government privatized two of its biggest banks in 2001 and, along with a large already-private bank, they were virtually unregulated. The banks expanded rapidly in Iceland and Western Europe, using borrowed money from abroad to make rafts of dubious investments. In early 2008, the banks had grown to the point that their deposits and loans amounted to eleven times Iceland's GDP. When the Icelandic banks began to run into liquidity shortfalls, they offered high interest rates for online accounts that attracted around 300,000 mostly English and Dutch depositors.

When all three banks hit the wall in the fall of 2008, there was no way in which the Icelandic government could bail them out. Instead, the government dissolved the three bankrupt banks, created three new entities to receive Icelandic deposits and loans, and directly negotiated with foreign creditors, who will receive less than their original investments. Iceland's currency (the krona) lost 58 percent in 2008, and in 2009 inflation rose to 19 percent and GDP sank 7 percent.

By the end of 2010, the vital signs of Iceland's economy were not only discernible, they were promising. But Iceland is not out of the woods; the British and Dutch governments had assumed the responsibility of insuring national depositors in the Icelandic bank and want Iceland to pay them back. The first negotiated agreement was defeated decisively by Iceland voters in a referendum in March 2010, and a renegotiated agreement was (gleefully) defeated in an April 2011 referendum. Iceland's desire to join the EU is, well, on hold. The IMF, in yet another new role, was involved in the negotiations for loans to Iceland, and there was some softening of its usual stance: the IMF allowed Iceland to impose capital controls and to run a fiscal deficit of 3 percent of GDP as a mild economic stimulus.

In 2008, when Ireland's real estate bubble burst, its biggest banks ran into trouble due to reckless real estate and other lending. The Irish government guaranteed the banks' depositors and their creditors, protecting depositors and those who lent money to the banks (bond holders) and transferring the entire burden to Ireland's taxpayers. This rash act thereby transformed a banking problem into a fiscal crisis. The government's commitment to the banks threatens a public debt of several times the size of Ireland's GDP.[1] Ireland had to submit to the humiliation of negotiating a rescue package from the European Central Bank, the European Commission, and the IMF.

Negotiators pressed Ireland hard on its low corporate tax rate, which brought in numerous foreign corporations, including Google and Yahoo, to establish outposts through which they could launder profits. Being a tax haven as well as allowing Irish banks to inflate a major domestic real estate bubble and to invest abroad in high-risk ventures created the illusion of a vibrant, growing economy, but they were not sound foundations. The corporate tax rate survived the negotiations, but the wreckage of the other two activities remains behind. As you can see from table 6.1, Ireland is not in good shape, and the ruling political party, with its unsavory connections to banks and bankers, was voted out of office for the first time in decades.

Ireland, unlike Iceland, is a member of the EU and of the eurozone, comprising 2 percent of eurozone GDP. Eurozone membership creates some barriers to the use of policies to recover from the downturn. The Irish do not have the ability to devalue its national currency in order to quickly lower wages and salaries across the board in terms of other currencies, stimulating its economy through increased exports and reduced imports. Nor can it increase its domestic money supply to lower interest rates and encourage domestic investment and consumption.

Devaluation and manipulating the domestic money supply require a national currency, and Ireland, along with everyone else in the eurozone, does not have a national currency. Ireland is welded into whatever is the value of the euro vis-à-vis other currencies, and it cannot expand its money supply without borrowing. One major advantage to membership in the eurozone, however, is that the Irish government has access to resources from the European Central Bank.

As noted, Ireland turned a banking crisis into a fiscal crisis by guaranteeing to meet its banks' obligations to depositors and creditors. But there is another set of eurozone countries in which this sequence is reversed: genuine fiscal crises with dire effects on banks. In the early 1990s, the introduction of the euro and low interest rates encouraged heavy borrowing by weaker economies, and money poured in from German banks and banks in other countries with low interest rates. The irresponsible borrowing led to a German export boom, but the end of real estate bubbles sharply reduced borrowing governments' tax revenues and ability to repay the loans.

Greece, Portugal, and Spain are the most problematic economies, and Italy and Belgium are often mentioned in the same paragraph.[2] Greece, like Ireland, received bailout loans from the Central Bank, the European Commission, and the International Monetary Fund in an agreement among them and the Greek government. The Greek population, however, has vociferously and at times violently declared its disagreement in the streets. Portugal received a $36.8 billion loan from the IMF in May 2011, and none of the highly indebted eurozone economies, so far, has defaulted.

Table 6.2 lists debt-to-GDP ratios for a selected number of countries. These are CIA estimates, and I've seen several different estimates for the United States. But of course we can trust the CIA.

These economies are stagnant or, as in the case of Ireland, continuing to contract; it is very unlikely that they are going to be able to close fiscal deficits or reduce national debts. Restructuring debt is increasingly likely—defaulting on the debt and negotiating with creditors to take a reduced proportion of the value of their bonds.[3] The fiscal deficit limit in the eurozone is supposed to be 3 percent of GDP, and the Greek and Irish bailouts stipulate this as a target even though larger and more prosperous eurozone members have often struggled to stay within the limit. Poland, which was the only one of the twenty-seven EU members to avoid recession during the recent financial crisis, is looking at an 8 percent deficit as the result of a recent economic slowdown that damaged tax revenues.

In much better shape than the peripheral eurozone countries, Turkey weathered the financial aspect of the crisis with little difficulty. Turkey had its own financial crisis in the early 2000s, and

Table 6.2. Public Debt Denominated in a Country's Home Currency as a Percentage of GDP (2010 Estimates) and Rankings for 42 of 132 Nations Selected

World Rank	Nation	Percentage of GDP	World Rank	Nation	Percentage of GDP
1	Japan	225.80	49	Malaysia	53.10
5	Greece	144.00	52	Pakistan	49.90
6	Iceland	123.80	54	Turkey	48.10
8	Italy	118.10	55	Norway	47.70
9	Singapore	102.40	56	Denmark	46.60
10	Belgium	98.60	59	Finland	45.40
11	Ireland	94.20	66	Mexico	41.50
14	France	83.50	69	Sweden	40.80
15	Portugal	83.20	72	Czech Republic	40.00
16	Egypt	80.50	86	Canada	34.00
18	Hungary	79.60	87	Taiwan	33.90
19	Germany	78.80	93	Indonesia	26.40
23	United Kingdom	76.50	99	New Zealand	25.50
24	Austria	70.40	103	South Korea	23.70
26	Netherlands	64.60	108	Australia	22.40
27	Spain	63.40	112	Hong Kong	18.20
31	Brazil	60.80	113	China	17.50
37	United States	58.90	114	Saudi Arabia	16.70
42	Vietnam	56.70	115	Iran	16.20
43	Philippines	56.50	123	Russia	9.50
45	India	55.90			
48	Poland	53.60	35	World	59.30

Source: Central Intelligence Agency, *The World Factbook*, https://www.cia.gov/library/publications/the-world-factbook/rankorder/2186rank.html (accessed Mar

in 2001 it reorganized its entire financial sector and reinstituted regulations and close monitoring. As a result, Turkish banks were sound, and the impact of the recession was translated to Turkey almost exclusively through the drop in the markets for its exports. It recovered fairly quickly as the larger EU members, its principal market, revived.

In 1995 Turkey became a member of the EU common market, but it still has not become a full member of the EU. The EU has reservations about Turkey's human rights record, especially about its suppression of the Kurdish separatist movement around the Iraqi border in the southeast. Another sticking point is that Turkey does not recognize the Greek Cypriot–dominated Republic of Cyprus, an EU member, and is the only nation to recognize the Turkish Cypriot–dominated Turkish Republic of Northern Cyprus. Turkish newspapers occasionally accuse EU officers of blatant religious discrimination, and EU newspapers occasionally wonder out loud whether Turkey is *really* European.

European or not, Turkey has been bolstered by its economic success and become a regional political and economic power that acts with independence from U.S. and EU foreign policies. This is particularly evident in its dealings with Iran and its coolness toward Israel. It's an interesting trajectory: a comparatively stable and democratic nation that may assume a major role in whatever comes out of the political unrest in the Middle East and North Africa. Its influence will no doubt be more positive than the influence of Saudi Arabia, which is severely frightened by the call to end rule by kings and dictators.

Returning to the eurozone, the name of the game is austerity. The idea is to cut back government spending and reduce debt sufficiently to reassure foreign creditors that the borrowing governments' bonds are creditworthy and to encourage private sectors to expand. Favorite types of budget cutting are reducing public workers' wages, salaries, health benefits, and pensions and increasing working hours and minimum retirement ages for all. These moves also have the advantage of lowering labor costs generally and enabling a nation to become more competitive in export markets and more attractive to foreign direct investment.

Germany has the largest population and economy in the eurozone and the EU. Although the German economy took a substantial hit from the 2008–2009 financial crisis and the decline in export demand, it rebounded well in most of 2010 with the help of a modest government stimulus and by managing to export almost half of its production. Although the German leadership is outspoken in criticizing the countries that cannot get their fiscal houses in order, there are a couple of unspoken facts. The first is that careless lending by German banks contributed to current sovereign debt crises. The second is that the weaknesses and uncertainties that plague the "periphery" of the eurozone have contributed to Germany's economic buoyancy by dragging the value of the euro below what it otherwise would have been in respect to the Japanese yen, enabling German machine and auto makers to undersell their most serious competitor. The euro's decline in respect to the U.S. dollar also helped Germany, especially since China's renminbi is tied to the U.S. dollar.

In the last decade, Germany pioneered backing away from Western Europe's traditionally generous worker benefits and social safety nets. While Germany's 7 percent unemployment is an eighteen-year low, German workers in the last decade have experienced a 4.5 percent decline in wages and salaries, diminished benefits, reduced job security, and an increase in the retirement age from 65 to 67 for those born after 1963. German workers are not happy with the general situation, believing that they have paid a high price for economic growth and resenting German taxpayers' having to bail out stumbling eurozone governments.

The process of shrinking social safety nets is always difficult, and demographic trends work against doing so. In the 1950s there were seven workers for every retiree in economically advanced societies, but by 2050, the ratio in the EU will be 1.3 to 1. The aging of the European population will shrink tax revenues at the very time that the demand for social expenditures will rise. Europeans' unwelcoming attitude toward immigrants limits the extent to which young workers from outside the EU can offset the trend. This will be especially difficult in France, where public social expenditures are currently 31 percent of the GDP, the highest in Europe. Only half of French workers work past the age of 50, and when the government raised the retirement age to 60, it brought thousands of protesters into the streets.

German workers' resentment about lending money to troubled eurozone countries underscores a major quandary for the eurozone. Although often compared to the United States, there is a key difference: there is no central political body in the eurozone with the legislative and fiscal powers of the U.S. federal government. If the U.S. Congress passed a bill that, in effect, used tax monies from California to spend in Mississippi, even if noticed by U.S. citizens, it would not be viewed as exceptional. Not so in the loose collection of semi-independent nations of the eurozone, where nationalist feelings are still strong after years of economic integration. A central bank is not enough.

Crisis conditions have renewed the debate over the desirability and feasibility of so tightly linking a batch of disparate nations with divergent political cultures and levels of inflation, employment, and fiscal deficits. Most doubters of the eurozone ("euroskeptics") come from outside the eurozone, and Germany and France continue to be unwavering supporters of the eurozone experiment.

Tensions among eurozone members are real and are not going away in the near future, but what seems to be the subject of too little debate is the European strategy being employed to overcome the Great Recession. The standard Keynesian advice would be to stimulate a national economy by *increasing* deficit expenditures with low interest rates to encourage borrowing for investment and consumption. The austerity program pursued by the European Central Bank has the classical imprint of the IMF, enhanced by chronic German fears of inflation. Pleasing international investors by reducing fiscal debt nicely complements greater export competitiveness by reducing the cost of national labor. These rationales for an assault on workers' rights and protections can be seen outside the eurozone; Great Britain and the United States (at both state and national levels) currently exhibit the same antiworker and antiunion sentiments under the twin banners of debt reduction and international competitiveness.

Recessionary policies leading to severe domestic recessions and high rates of unemployment can accomplish lower labor costs, as demonstrated by the 10 to 15 percent wage reductions achieved by Estonia, Lithuania, and Latvia. These examples also demonstrate how nasty and extended such a program can be, and even if successful in lowering domestic prices and wages, the hard-currency debts are not reduced. But a prior question is whether such policies can stimulate the economies that are implementing them. The logic is dubious, the historical record

says no, and recent events vote against it. The German stimulation package ran out in the fourth quarter of 2010, and the
mildly austere budget slowed economic growth. Unlike the
United States, which had a larger and longer-lasting stimulus,
Germany's GDP is still below prerecession levels. Great Britain's
Conservative government implemented a much more austere
budget in the name of fiscal responsibility and succeeded in
reversing Britain's slow recovery in the fourth quarter of 2010.

If the EU and the United States are unwilling to stimulate
their economies in systematic and coordinated ways, it is unclear how they will regain the path to steady growth and toler-
able levels of unemployment.

Asia and Elsewhere in the Race from the Bottom

If the rhetoric of recent G20 meetings of the finance ministers and
central bankers of the twenty leading economies is to be believed,
China is hoped to be the principal source of the tide expected
to lift all boats. After all, China is the world's second-largest
economy, behind the United States, and it has demonstrated the
ability to grow at astounding rates for more than a decade at a
time. Although the value of its imports lags behind the value of
its exports, its imports of raw materials and some manufactured
components of its export production are major factors behind the
growth of East Asian and Southeast Asian economies. This influence has also begun to be felt in Latin America, South Asia, and
Africa, where Chinese firms are forever on the lookout for natural
resources to feed into their manufacturing sector.

China, along with most of the Asian economies, was not as
exposed as Europe to the toxic financial instruments produced
by the U.S. financial sector. As we mentioned in the last chapter,
the Asian nations' running balance-of-trade surpluses did invest
large amounts in U.S. securities, but they favored less-risky U.S.
Treasury notes over the higher-yielding CDOs. As a result, the
downturn was transmitted to the Asian economies principally
through declines in demand for their exports. Aided by a mas-

sive stimulus in the form of infrastructure investments, China bounced back rather quickly from the initial blow in late 2008.

But there are some factors of the Chinese economy that should be looked at more closely, because they concern China's ability to be the savior of the international economy. Not only are the United States and China the world's two largest economies, they are, respectively, the world's largest trade deficit nation and the world's largest trade surplus nation. China lends much of this surplus to the United States, which is, well, unusual: a nation with a per capita income around $3,000 is lending billions of dollars to a nation with a per capita income of almost $50,000. The February 2011 G20 meeting, over Chinese objections, took a first step toward monitoring such imbalances that constitute a potential source of instability.

Some of China's megatrade surpluses are the result of the Chinese government's deliberate policy of keeping the value of their currency—the renminbi—at a level below what it would be if it were genuinely to float. This action keeps the price of Chinese exports in foreign currencies lower than they would otherwise be and discourages imports into China. The Chinese government has been under strong international pressure, especially from the United States, to change this practice, and in the middle of 2010, the Chinese government allowed the renminbi to appreciate over 12 percent. While not a stunning change, if the combination of Chinese inflation and government changes in the peg persist for two or three years, the renminbi will have appreciated the needed 20 to 30 percent necessary for a more healthful trade balance.

The EU has its own concerns about its trade deficit with China, but they are taking a policy course different from the United States. The EU accuses the Chinese government of unfairly subsidizing a number of its export producers, and in May 2011 the EU imposed the first antisubsidy tariff against imports of coated paper used in magazines and brochures. They imply that there will be additional such tariffs when they uncover evidence of subsidies in other branches of manufacturing.

A fascinating recent development is that China is developing a labor shortage. "Chinese labor shortage" sounds like an oxymoron, but China has experienced such rapid and sustained growth in export-oriented production that employers are beginning to run into shortages and are having to raise wages and improve working conditions. Another sign of this is that Chinese workers have pulled off two highly publicized and successful strikes, and while these strikes were at foreign-owned firms—and Japanese at that—they show that times are changing.

On the labor-supply side, there are a number of factors constraining the pool of able and willing workers. The Chinese government's efforts to improve the lives of the rural poor in inland and western provinces have had some success and thus dampened young people's eagerness to migrate to coastal factory jobs. And there are fewer fifteen- to twenty-five-year-olds, due to China's one-child policy that began affecting family sizes a little more than twenty years ago. Finally, more young people than ever are attending college rather than joining factory workforces.

These two pressures—the slowly rising value of the renminbi and rising wages—are increasing domestic production costs and export prices in foreign markets and pulling down profit margins that are already low due to the bargaining power of big retailers like Target and Walmart that shop the world. Chinese firms are responding to these changes in two principal ways. One is to go to lower-wage areas, and Vietnam is frequently mentioned in this regard. The second is to shift production in the direction of up-market products where profit margins are greater. In apparel, this has meant supplying The Gap and Liz Claiborne rather than Walmart, or shifting from shoes made of synthetic materials to high-quality leather shoes. In addition, it means continuing to shift aggressively into new export products like electronics, automobiles, and other sophisticated products that have higher profit margins. If this trend continues, China will be competing more with South Korea and Southern Europe instead of Thailand and Indonesia and thus replicating the experience of post–World War II Japan and South Korea.

A third strategy, which is too inchoate to call a trend, is expanding China's domestic markets for its goods. This might involve some seismic shifts in the distribution of income and in the provision of social services (e.g., health and education). Although this strategy is politically riskier than working up the export food chain, it appears to have at least rhetorical support among China's leadership.

One last observation about China's economic growth uplifting the international economy is that Chinese leaders are clearly thinking seriously about slowing down China's rate of economic growth. The appreciation of the renminbi in 2010 and the recent decision to increase interest rates are both policies that suggest that the leadership believe it would not be in China's interest to continue to grow at such a breakneck pace, which was greater in 2010 than had been planned. Domestic inflation, labor shortages, workers' job actions, supply-chain bottlenecks, and increasing awareness of the severity of environmental damage all point to the desirability of a more moderate pace of growth, which may reduce China's ability to reinvigorate the world economy.

These reservations are reasonable, but China's economic buoyancy did help recovery in the East and Southeast Asian economies. In addition, China's resurgence was felt throughout the world's resource exporters, including Russia, Canada, New Zealand, and Australia, as well as parts of Latin America and Africa. China's imports of manufactured goods, however, have done little for the industrialized nations, including Japan, which for almost two decades has been trying to counter strong pulls toward deflation and stagnation. Japan's rapidly aging population poses challenges, and political fracturing rather like that of the United States hinders the development and implementation of effective policy solutions.

Japan's chronic problems were eclipsed by the 9.0 earthquake and tsunami of March 2011 that destroyed so much of northeastern Japan, a human disaster with implications for the

Japanese and global economies. Stabilization of the damaged Fukushima Daiichi nuclear plant and easy access of essential food and housing for the survivors are the first orders of business before reconstruction can begin. Commentators are divided on whether the reconstruction will stimulate or strain the Japanese economy, which does have underutilized capacity. While Japan possesses large reserves of foreign currency heavily invested in U.S. Treasury bonds, Japan also possesses a national debt of more than twice the size of its GDP. This is not as serious as it might seem at first, because 95 percent of that debt is held domestically and all of it is denominated in yen, which the government can print.

This last point distinguishes Japan from the troubled eurozone economies of Greece, Ireland, Portugal, and Spain. The G7 ministers and central bankers of the world industrial leaders have promised to intervene in currency markets to minimize the appreciation of the yen expected as a result of Japan's repatriating a portion of their foreign investments to finance reconstruction, an appreciation that would hinder the recovery of the Japanese economy. In the broader scheme of things, Japan supplies electronics, adhesives, and many components for foreign firms. One General Motors truck plant in Louisiana closed within weeks of the natural disasters because of parts shortages, and Volvo in Sweden and Toyota transplants in Ohio are expecting to experience shortages.

India was less exposed to international product markets than China and Japan, and it did not take as strong a hit in 2008–2009. Indian politicians continue to speak about further major reform, such as opening its markets to foreign direct investment, but it still is difficult for foreign firms to do business in India. Because of corruption and especially the multitude of rules and regulations, India has much less foreign direct investment than one would expect in a country that has more than a billion people and that grows 8 to 9 percent a year. For example, Walmart has been trying to establish a foothold in the Indian retail market for a couple of years, but to do so, it would have to be granted a waiver from rules that protect the thousands, probably millions, of small retail stores throughout the country.

These rules are criticized roundly, and not only in Bentonville, Arkansas. Indian consumers would no doubt experience cheaper retail prices if Walmart, Target, and other companies were let in. On the other hand, there is a chance that by going slowly, Indian retail markets could be opened up only after there were alternative employments for displaced shopkeepers. This would significantly dilute the socially wrenching and politically dangerous impact of such a change. The persistence of such rules may be due to bureaucratic inertia, political pressure, and corruption rather than deliberate choice, but no matter its source, the result is a measured and manageable pace of change with minimum disruption. In this respect, India is not unlike some East Asian nations, although India has not embraced the full-scale export-platform model of growth.

Recent rises in oil prices may also dampen the recovery of the global economy. Much of the current price rises are responses to the uncertainties of the political situations in North Africa and the Middle East. At this writing in March 2011, popular protests have forced President Zine el-Abidine Ben Ali of Tunisia and President Hosni Mubarak of Egypt, both secular autocrats actively supported by U.S. foreign policy, out of office. In addition to serious turbulence in Algeria, Jordan, and Iraq, Muammar al-Qaddafi of Libya and President Ali Abdullah Saleh of Yemen are both under heavy siege by popular protests. In the case of Qaddafi, European and U.S. bombardments have added pressure, supposedly to protect Libyan civilians from Qaddifi's violent retaliation. In Bahrain, however, when national security forces backed up by Saudi Arabian troops violently assaulted protesters, there was little reaction in the West. The protesters were advocating greater political and economic rights for the Shia majority against a Sunni royal family, and Saudi Arabia and the United States are both nervous about Iran, mostly Shia. In addition, the U.S. policy is consistently deferential to Saudi Arabia, the world's largest exporter of oil. Interesting times.

Along with petroleum, prices for aluminum, copper, magnesium, some agricultural crops, and other primary products have also risen, energizing a number of Latin American economies. In the late 1990s and early 2000s, most neoliberal governments in Latin America were displaced by leftist or at least "progressive" forces supported by inclusive political mobilizations. The repudiation of the Washington Consensus included blocking the Bush administration's Free Trade Area of the Americas, instead expanding Mercosur, and led to a (slight) reduction in poverty and a renewal of social policies.

Brazil has been especially dynamic in regional politics. Brazilian initiatives led to the formation of new regional alliances that successfully defused what could have become a war between Ecuador and Colombia, resolved an Ecuadorian police strike with dangerous potential, and mobilized regional governments in defense of democracy to block a coup d'état against the Bolivian president. The new organizations have eclipsed the U.S.-dominated Organization of American States.

Africa also has received benefits from growing Asian markets and high primary-product prices, and China has been aggressively seeking resource-based products throughout Africa and either buying the output of local mines and farms or, in an unprecedented manner, using foreign direct investment to secure commodity production and export. The Chinese prime minister predicted that the value of trade between China and sub-Saharan Africa in 2010 would prove to be $100 billion, having increased by a factor of ten in the decade. If this prediction holds, China will have become sub-Saharan Africa's largest trading partner, having overtaken Europe and the United States.

Chinese foreign direct investment in Africa has resulted in eight hundred state-run Chinese companies operating in Africa toward the end of the 2000s, and in their wake has come a multitude of independent Chinese immigrants who have established all sorts of services, shops, and small-scale manufacturing enterprises that sell to Africans as well as to Chinese firms' employees. Chinese contractors are said to be winning 50 percent of public works projects in Africa, and Chinese lending to African states has surpassed IMF and World Bank lending to Africa. The Chinese are not operating alone in Africa; they have strong competition for African products and investment opportunities, especially from Russian, Brazilian, and Indian firms.

The Chinese declare a principle of noninterference in other governments' affairs, a stance that enables them to do business with some of the regions' leaders with records of consistent human rights violations and corruption. Sudan (oil) and the Democratic Republic of Congo (copper) are examples. The latter is an eight billion dollar Chinese purchase of 68 percent of the state-owned copper company and includes the Chinese building three highways, a railway, health clinics, and universities.

The boom in primary-product prices has some dangers. After all, Latin America and Africa have been primary-product exporters since the nineteenth century, and what was essentially a colonial model of exporting primary products and importing manufactured products failed to propel the regions into consistent economic growth with widespread benefits. Even Brazil's impressive array of manufactured exports is being overwhelmed by China's seemingly insatiable demand for soy and iron ore. Whether or not the most recent commodity boom gets translated into long-term benefits to the regions' populations is a matter of politics and policies, not free markets.

China's economy is indeed coming back, energized by massive public investments in infrastructure projects. China's rebound is helping economic recoveries in Southeast Asia and resource-based export economies in Africa and Latin America. Some of this positive effect will increase exports from the metropolitan nations, but whether China's dynamism will be sufficient to bring these economies out of the morass of the Great Recession is an open question.

The answer to that question is likely to be no if the United States and the EU persist in policies of austerity, seemingly determined to reverse their stuttering recoveries. The U.S. legislature and electorate are fully capable of generating paralyzing gridlock, and the EU and especially the eurozone have so many contradictory interests that Germany's assertion of conservative leadership is tenuous. Even if the German austere path to EU recovery prevails, high costs borne by the most vulnerable in the population are more certain than general economic recovery.

Competitive capitalism is capable of generating vigorous bursts of economic expansion and dire contractions, but there is an irony here somewhere. The most blatant demonstration of international capitalism's penchant for self-destruction has not provoked sweeping new coordinated restrictions and limitations on free-trade global capitalism in order to contain its harmful potential and to protect those adversely affected. In a perverse manner, the Great Recession seems to be bringing forth a set of policies closely related to what the Washington Consensus imposed on mostly Latin American debtor nations in the 1980s, creating the lost decade and the erosion of organized labor's political and economic standing. The late 2000s are also similar to the 1980s in that governments and taxpayers are once again picking up after the destruction wrought by powerful banks' voracious and myopic quest for profits, but they are different in that policies friendly to international capital are being implemented in metropolitan governments formerly less susceptible to capital's agenda. As in the 1980s, the results have been to reward those who created the crisis and punish those who are its principal victims.

In the most dramatic fashion, financial markets in particular have demonstrated their inability to correct themselves and function in a manner that supports economic prosperity beyond the salaries, bonuses, and capital gains of a select few. With a worldwide labor surplus, employers, representing capital, are in the saddle, and workers are on the defensive. In line with classical liberalism, neoliberals represent the market as the realm of freedom and government policy as the realm of coercion. Since free markets mean freedom for capital to operate without considering anything other than private gain, market freedoms are indeed liberating for those whose wealth and exercise of power had been constrained by government policy. On the other hand, free markets can be debilitating for those whose standards of living depend on workers' rights and the provision of public services. The consequence is increasingly polarized societies.

Notes

Chapter 1: The Twentieth-Century
Quest for a Stable International Economy

1. The gross national product (GNP) is a nation's total annual production of goods and services. To be consistent with other nations' accounting practices, the U.S. government adopted gross domestic product (GDP) as the most aggregated income account in February 1991. The only significant difference between the two measures is net income from international investments.

Chapter 3: U.S. Political Shifts and
beyond Bretton Woods, 1970s to 1980s

1. For this purpose, I have included the white populations of the eleven former Confederate states plus Kentucky, Missouri, and Oklahoma.

2. The irony, of course, was that the United States had simply replaced France in 1954 when France was militarily defeated trying to reclaim its former colony of Vietnam.

Chapter 4: The New International Economy and the Dissolution of U.S. Modern Times, 1970s to 1990s

1. Instead of regarding public workers' benefits as models for what all workers should have, the political effort is to have them participate in a race to the bottom. Taxes are especially resented in the United States.

2. I am grateful to Damien W. S. Weaver for forcing the importance of these connections on me.

Chapter 5: The Triumph of Free-Market Global Capitalism, 1990s to 2007

1. Cuba has the potential for a similar disaster. If the same institutional "reforms" were wreaked on Cuba, as many prominent in U.S. politics would have it, the Cuban Revolution's unusual degree of income equality and world-class health and education systems would be out the window.

2. These common markets should not be confused with two international organizations often in the news. The Organisation for Economic Co-operation and Development (OECD) is composed of thirty of the world's richest nations for the purposes of coordinating policies and fostering mutually beneficial agreements on a range of issues. The Group of Seven (G7) is a loosely knit club of seven of the largest economic powers with pretty much the same agenda as the OECD. With the admission of Russia in 1997, the G7 became the G8. China may be admitted before long, and India and Brazil are in the queue for membership. There is also a G20 that includes the most prosperous two-thirds of the OECD. Clear?

3. NAFTA formally began on January 1, 1994, which is the same day that the Zapatistas in the southern Mexican state of Chiapas declared themselves to the world and began the process of "liberating" parts of Chiapas. The timing was not accidental.

4. The year 2008 is the beginning of the Great Recession, but I use it for the table because unlike 2009 the export figures had yet to decline and the full impact on GDPs was still to be felt.

5. The index and its critics can be found at http://www .foreignpolicy.com/articles/2010/06/21/2010_failed_states_ index_interactive_map_ and_rankings.

Chapter 6: The Twenty-First-Century Quest for a Stable International Economy

1. A fiscal deficit is the shortfall between governmental revenues and expenditures in a year, while the national debt (sometimes called public debt or sovereign debt) is the accumulation of all deficits—the amount of government bonds in the hands of creditors.

2. Wall Street was not an innocent bystander: Goldman Sachs and Morgan Stanley helped Greece and Italy use exotic financial instruments to hide the extent of their debts from investors and the European Union.

3. Angela Merkel, the German chancellor, favors that investors take a "haircut" as a condition for extending bailout loans. Greece, Spain, and Portugal are adamantly against this because it would raise investors' risks and therefore the cost of borrowing money.

Selected Readings and Websites

This list of books includes a few readings on a variety of subjects that I explore in the book. I do not agree with everything in all of them, or perhaps in any of them, but they are serious and interesting efforts to come to grips with important issues. Some of them are classics in their fields and others illustrate how scholars at the time were wrestling with the emergence of new practices and relationships. All of them, however, are smart, provocative, and worth reading in their own right.

I have grouped the readings according to my chapters, that is, chronologically, but the books in the first group have such broad scopes that they go beyond the combinations of chapters that I have used to develop the groupings.

General

Block, Fred L. *The Origins of International Economic Disorder: A Study of the United States International Monetary Policy from World War II to the Present.* Berkeley: University of California Press, 1996.

Brenner, Robert. *The Economics of Global Turbulence: The Advanced Capitalist Economies from Long Boom to Long Downturn, 1945–2005.* New York: Verso, 2006.

Engerman, Stanley L., and Robert E. Gallman, eds. *The Cambridge Economic History of the United States*. Vol. 3, *The Twentieth Century*. New York: Cambridge University Press, 2000.

Frieden, Jeffrey A. *Global Capitalism: Its Fall and Rise in the Twentieth Century*. New York: Norton, 2006.

Gilpin, Robert. *The Challenge of Global Capitalism: The World Economy in the 21st Century*. Princeton, NJ: Princeton University Press, 2000.

Chapter 1

Go, Julian. *American Empire and the Politics of Meaning: Elite Political Cultures in the Philippines and Puerto Rico during U.S. Colonialism*. Durham, NC: Duke University Press, 2008.

Gordon, Colin. *New Deals: Business, Labor, and Politics in America, 1920–1935*. New York: Cambridge University Press, 1994.

Kindleberger, Charles P. *The World in Depression, 1929–1939*. Rev. ed. Berkeley: University of California Press, 1986.

Lipsitz, George. *Rainbow at Midnight: Labor and Culture in the 1940s*. Urbana: University of Illinois Press, 1994.

Love, Eric T. *Race over Empire: Racism and U.S. Imperialism, 1865–1900*. Chapel Hill: University of North Carolina Press, 2004.

Montgomery, David. *The Fall of the House of Labor: The Workplace, the State, and American Worker Activism, 1865–1925*. New York: Cambridge University Press, 1987.

Sanders, Elizabeth. *Roots of Reform: Farmers, Workers and the American State, 1877–1917*. Chicago: University of Chicago Press, 1999.

Strom, Sharon Hartman. *Beyond the Typewriter: Gender, Class, and the Origins of Modern American Office Work, 1900–1930*. Urbana: University of Illinois Press, 1992.

Stromquist, Shelton. *Reinventing "The People": The Progressive Movement, the Class Problem, and the Origins of Modern Liberalism*. Urbana: University of Illinois Press, 2006.

Chapters 2 and 3

Bergsten, C. Fred, Thomas Horst, and Theodore H. Moran. *American Multinationals and American Interests*. Washington, DC: Brookings Institution, 1978.

Braverman, Harry. *Labor and Monopoly Capital: The Degradation of Work in the Twentieth Century*. 2nd ed. New York: Monthly Review Press, 1998.

Chandler, Alfred D. *The Visible Hand: The Managerial Revolution in American Business*. Cambridge, MA: Belknap, 1977.

Coontz, Stephanie. *The Way We Never Were: American Families and the Nostalgia Trap*. New York: Basic Books, 1992.

Friedland, William H., Amy E. Barton, and Robert J. Thomas. *Manufacturing Green Gold: Capital, Labor, and Technology in the Lettuce Industry*. New York: Cambridge University Press, 1981.

Gordon, Colin. *New Deals, Business, Labor, and Politics in America, 1920–1935*. New York: Cambridge University Press, 1994.

Gordon, David M., Richard Edwards, and Michael Reich. *Segmented Work, Divided Workers: The Historical Transformation of Labor in the United States*. New York: Cambridge University Press, 1994.

Williamson, John. "What Washington Means by Policy Reform." In *Latin American Adjustment: How Much Has Happened*? edited by John Williamson, 7–17. Washington, DC: Institute for International Economics, 1990.

Chapters 4 through 6

Amsden, Alice H. *Escape from Empire: The Developing World's Journey through Heaven and Hell*. Cambridge: MIT Press, 2007.

Dowd, Douglas Fitzgerald. *Inequality and the Global Economic Crisis*. New York: Pluto, 2009.

Evans, Peter. *Embedded Autonomy: States and Industrial Transformation*. Princeton, NJ: Princeton University Press, 1995.

Gereffi, Gary, and Donald L. Wyman, eds. *Manufacturing Miracles: Paths of Industrialization in Latin America and East Asia.* Princeton, NJ: Princeton University Press, 1994.

Greenhouse, Steven. *The Big Squeeze: Tough Times for American Workers.* New York: Alfred A. Knopf, 2008.

Grunwald, Joseph, and Kenneth Flamm. *The Global Factory: Foreign Assembly in International Trade.* Washington, DC: Brookings Institution, 1985.

Kotz, David M., Terrence McDonough, and Michael Reich. *Social Structures of Accumulation: The Political Economy of Growth and Crisis.* New York: Cambridge University Press, 1994.

McDonough, Terrence, Michael Reich, and David Kotz. *Contemporary Capitalism and Its Crises: Social Structures of Accumulation Theory for the 21st Century.* New York: Cambridge University Press, 2010.

Panagariya, Arvid. *India: The Emerging Giant.* New York: Oxford University Press, 2008.

Paus, Eva, ed. *Global Capitalism Unbound: Winners and Losers from Offshore Outsourcing.* New York: Palgrave Macmillan, 2007.

Pereira, Luiz Carlos Bresser. *Developing Brazil: Overcoming the Failure of the Washington Consensus.* Boulder, CO: Lynne Rienner, 2009.

Standing, Guy. "Global Feminization through Flexible Labor." *World Development* 17 (1989): 1077–95.

Stiglitz, Joseph E. *Freefall: America, Free Markets, and the Sinking of the World Economy.* New York: W. W. Norton, 2010.

———. *Globalization and Its Discontents.* New York: W. W. Norton, 2002.

Strayer, Robert W. *Why Did the Soviet Union Collapse? Understanding Historical Change.* New York: M. E. Sharpe, 1998.

Websites

Here is a short list of websites that you may consult for additional information and understanding about national and international economic affairs. I have used all of them, so I can recommend them for their accuracy and ease of use. On the other hand, it would be difficult to characterize the prose of all but a couple of these sites as graceful and spirited.

U.S. Government Data

http://www.census.gov/compendia/statab/
The Statistical Abstract of the United States is the most comprehensive compilation of general data. Since the tables appear to have been scanned into the website, they can be difficult to read, and because the data are assembled annually, they are not current. Nevertheless, *The Statistical Abstract* is a good place to begin looking for economic information because each one contains excellent guides to data sources.

http://www.bea.gov
The home page of the U.S. Department of Commerce, Bureau of Economic Analysis, offers the most complete and current economic information, domestic and international. The *Survey of Current Business* is their monthly publication, which can be accessed through a link on the left of the BEA home page. Each issue of the survey includes valuable articles on different aspects of U.S. economic activity as well as a standard set of tables of current and historical data.

http://www.federalreserve.gov
This is the home page of the board of governors of the Federal Reserve System, and it has a wide range of current data and analyses that are easy to access. One of the useful features of this website is that it can connect you to all twelve regional Federal Reserve Banks. In the search window (on the top right), type in "district banks." The first search result is this: FRB: Federal Reserve Districts and Banks. Click on that link, and it will take you to a map and list of links to the regional banks. My favorites are the analyses available from the Boston and Chicago banks, but you should poke around the one in your

area for good information about your region and analyses of local and national issues.

http://www.bls.gov
This is the website of the U.S. Department of Labor, Bureau of Labor Statistics. There are a lot of data there with a particular focus on the characteristics of the U.S. labor force. It is also the principal source of information about the consumer price index. The site can be confusing to use.

http://www.minneapolisfed.org/research/data/us/
I recommend this site of the Minneapolis Federal Reserve Bank for a website with clear labels and links that has a good exposition of the consumer price index and other financial data.

General Business News and Views

The *Economist* and the *Wall Street Journal* require subscriptions to access their online editions. *Financial Times* (http://www. ft.com) and the *New York Times* (http://www.nytimes.com) allow limited access to current stories at no cost. Both are good, but the *New York Times* business section is my favorite; it is clear, timely, and often irreverent.

http://www.bloomberg.com
The articles are concise, informative, and appear to have no particular axe to grind.

http://www.thenation.com
The *Nation* magazine has a subtitle: "Unconventional Wisdom since 1865." That is an accurate description of the magazine and the website, which does not respect artificial distinctions between "politics" and "economics." It also has interesting and provocative coverage of cultural trends. Closely associated with the *Nation*, Tom Engelhardt produces a free e-mail newsletter from tomdispatch@nationinstitute.org as "a regular antidote to the mainstream media." It's worth looking at.

International

http://www.worldbank.org
The World Bank home page is interesting and well designed. Hit "Data" and "Research" at the top of the page for a rich variety of data and analyses.

http://www.imf.org
The IMF home page contains a large number of easily navigated links to current issues and international financial data.

http://jolis.worldbankimflib.org
This is the site of the World Bank-IMF Joint Library. You can search the catalogue by using the JOLIS search box.

http://www.hoover.org
The Hoover Institution—a conservative think tank on the Stanford University campus—offers extensive and critical studies of the IMF.

https://www.cia.gov/library/publications/the-world-factbook/
The CIA *World Factbook* is a useful source of once-over-lightly information about individual nations.

http://www.oecd.org/home/
The Organisation for Economic Co-operation and Development (OECD) has thirty-four members of mostly European and North American nations, but its focus is truly global. It has timely articles listed on the home page, and there are links to its extensive data banks at the bottom of the home page.

Index

About the Author

Frederick S. Weaver is professor emeritus of economics and history at Hampshire College. His most recent books are *Economic Literacy: Basic Economics with an Attitude*, Third Edition (2011), and, with Sharon Hartman Strom, *Confederates in the Tropics: Charles Swett's Travelogue of 1868* (2011).